Ohio's
Lake Erie
Public Access Guidebook

Ohio Department of Natural Resources
Office of Coastal Management
105 West Shoreline Drive
Sandusky, OH 44870

Publication Date: 2010

This document was prepared by the Ohio Department of Natural Resources Office of Coastal Management under award NA08NOS4190434 from the National Oceanic and Atmospheric Administration, U.S. Department of Commerce through the Ohio Department of Natural Resources, Office of Coastal Management. The statements, findings, conclusions and recommendations are those of the author(s) and do not necessarily reflect the views of the National Oceanic and Atmospheric Administration, U.S. Department of Commerce.

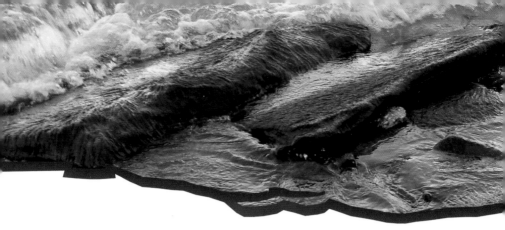

Contents

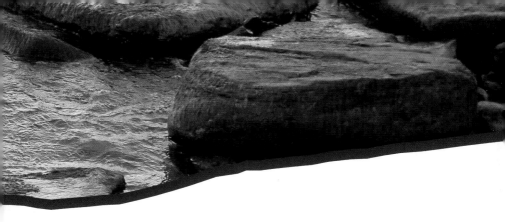

Ohio Department of Natural Resources Office of Coastal Management

Mission: Achieve a balance between use and preservation of Lake Erie's coastal resources, in collaboration with our partners, by effectively administering the Ohio Coastal Management Program.

Learn more: ohiodnr.com/coastal

Guiding Exploration

of Ohio's 312-mile Lake Erie Shore

The *Lake Erie Public Access Guidebook* provides a comprehensive, user-friendly resource for exploring the recreational and scenic public sites bordering Lake Erie – even ones that may not be marked on a road map or programmed in a global positioning device. From well-known favorites to simple, secret treasures along the shore, the *Lake Erie Public Access Guidebook* maps all known sites, outlines each site's amenities and serves as a tool to help you discover the perfect spot to spend your day... or even your week.

The Ohio Department of Natural Resources (ODNR) Office of Coastal Management (OCM) created this book and the online companion website to encourage exploration of Ohio's shore and to fulfill duties assigned in Ohio Revised Code §1506 and the federally approved Ohio Coastal Management Program.

ORC §1506.05: *"The director of natural resources shall prepare and maintain a current inventory of public access facilities and areas for the Ohio shoreline of Lake Erie, including, without limitation, shoreline parks, cultural resources, natural areas, wildlife refuges, harbors of refuge, boat launch ramps, shoreline fishing areas and beaches."*

Policy 21 of the Ohio Coastal Management Program: *"It is the policy of the state of Ohio to provide lakeshore recreational opportunities and public access and encourage tourism along Lake Erie."*

Excitement for Everyone

From a nature lover's pursuit of peaceful tranquility at a preserve, to a family's rambunctious day of splashing at the beach, Ohio's coastal splendors have much to offer.

The environments along Ohio's 312-mile Lake Erie shore range from lush wetlands and a Western Basin island archipelago to a Central Basin with impressive dunes and high shale bluffs. The shore boasts pristine natural sand beaches, cobble beaches, dunes, estuaries and many constructed points of interest including commercial and recreational harbors, industrial ports and fishing piers.

Stretching from Toledo to Conneaut, Ohio has 164 public access sites along Lake Erie, which total nearly 53 miles of publicly accessible shore. The 53 miles are approximately 17 percent of Ohio's coast and collectively account for over 15,000 acres.

Public access sites include state, city, village and township parks; county metropark preserves and reservations; state and local nature preserves; state wildlife areas; public cemeteries; memorials and monuments; lighthouses; dead-end road rights-of-way and scenic vistas.

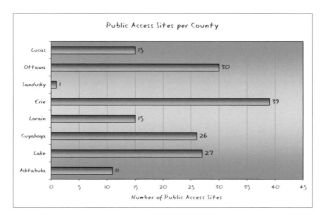

This guidebook does not include sites that are private such as individual homes, beach associations or clubs, commercial or private marinas or airports, amusement parks, restaurants, museums, golf courses, campgrounds, retail plazas, industrial facilities, apartment or condominium complexes or mobile home parks.

Note that many public access sites listed in this guidebook are adjacent to residential, commercial and industrial properties. Nuisance behavior or trespassing may be subject to prosecution.

Data Collection and Sources

Information in the *Lake Erie Public Access Guidebook* was collected by the ODNR Office of Coastal Management between 2005 and 2009. The primary data collection method was through fieldwork, supplemented by these other sources:

- Parcel data from coastal county auditors.
- ODNR Division of Real Estate and Land Management's 2008 *Statewide Comprehensive Outdoor Recreation Program* (SCORP) data.
- ODNR Division of Watercraft's 2004 Boating Access data.
- The state of Ohio's 2006 Statewide Imagery Program aerial photography.
- County and local maps.
- Orthometric photography
- Internet resources

In 2009, coastal staff verified locations and amenities with local officials, including recreation directors, public works and service departments, park managers and other local authorities. As a result, some sites were excluded from the public access inventory and other sites were added.

Amenities Legend

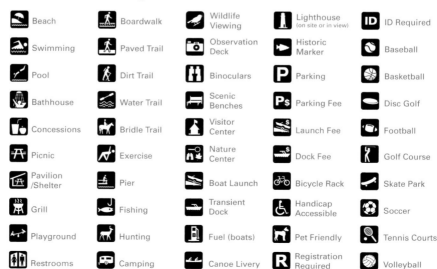

Beach	Boardwalk	Wildlife Viewing	Lighthouse (on site or in view)	ID Required
Swimming	Paved Trail	Observation Deck	Historic Marker	Baseball
Pool	Dirt Trail	Binoculars	Parking	Basketball
Bathhouse	Water Trail	Scenic Benches	Parking Fee	Disc Golf
Concessions	Bridle Trail	Visitor Center	Launch Fee	Football
Picnic	Exercise	Nature Center	Dock Fee	Golf Course
Pavilion /Shelter	Pier	Boat Launch	Bicycle Rack	Skate Park
Grill	Fishing	Transient Dock	Handicap Accessible	Soccer
Playground	Hunting	Fuel (boats)	Pet Friendly	Tennis Courts
Restrooms	Camping	Canoe Livery	Registration Required	Volleyball

How to Use the Guidebook

The Lake Erie Public Access Guidebook is divided into nine chapters – an introductory chapter and one chapter for each of Ohio's coastal counties. The county chapters, arranged geographically from west to east, are: Lucas, Ottawa, Sandusky, Erie, Lorain, Cuyahoga, Lake and Ashtabula. Within each chapter, mainland public access sites are arranged geographically from west to east; island sites are arranged clockwise by island.

Pages include a brief description about each site, a symbolical listing of that location's amenities, a location map, pictures and contact information to learn more about the destination. The key to identify the symbols used to represent amenities and services, and a map legend, are found below.

General information about each coastal county, the Ohio Coastal Management Program, Office of Coastal Management and common Lake Erie activities including fishing, hunting, boating, swimming and beach safety tips are found in this introductory chapter.

The Office of Coastal Management has made every effort to ensure that the Lake Erie Public Access Guidebook is error free. If you discover any inaccuracies/ exclusions or have general comments, please contact coastal staff at:

ODNR Office of Coastal Management
ATTN: Public Access Guidebook Comments
105 West Shoreline Drive, Sandusky, OH 44870
Tel: 419-626-7980   Toll Free: 1-888-OhioCMP
Email: coastal@dnr.state.oh.us

Map Legend

X Public Access Site	Trail (Not all trails shown)
x Adjacent/Nearby Public Access Site	Water Trail
Water	X Water Trail Access Point
90 Interstate Route	Municipal Street
6 US Route	Private Road
83 State Route	Park Road
County Road	Highway Ramp
Township Road	Lake Erie Coastal Ohio Trail (Orange buffer around road)

Office of Coastal Management

Coastal management is a continuous dynamic process by which actions are taken for the sustainable use, development and protection of our shared coastal resources. In Ohio, coastal management's importance lies in Lake Erie, a socially, economically and environmentally significant natural resource.

Ohio's portion of the Lake Erie Watershed, 11,649 square miles, drains all or portions of 35 Ohio counties and is home to 4.65 million residents. An estimated 2.6 million people reside in Ohio's eight coastal counties; 3 million Ohioans tap Lake Erie as their source of daily drinking water.

Ohio's Lake Erie watershed includes large and small businesses and industries, world-class institutes of higher-education, welcoming communities, prime farmland, scenic rivers, lush forests, natural wetlands, growing sand dunes and thriving estuaries. According to 2008 study*, visitors to Ohio's Lake Erie region spend $10.7 billion annually. This includes the estimated impact of Ohio's Lake Erie sportfishing which was $801 million in 2006**.

To help balance the uses of resources with sustaining a healthy environment, the ODNR Office of Coastal Management (OCM) administers the federally approved Ohio Coastal Management Program (OCMP). The program sets forth policies and guidelines to monitor activities that affect coastal resources and ensure resource protection while balancing economic, cultural and environmental interests for the benefit it of all citizens and future generations. The Ohio Coastal Management Program Document can be downloaded from the Office of Coastal Management website: ohiodnr.com/coastal.

Our Activities Include:

- **Implementing laws, regulations and voluntary programs** to help achieve the goal of attaining and sustaining a healthy coast and lake by balancing use and conservation. OCM involvement includes reviewing applications for Coastal Erosion Area Permits, Shore Structure Permits, Submerged Land Leases and other regulatory authorities as outlined in Ohio Revised Code §1506 and Ohio Administrative Code §1501-6. OCM is also helping to draft rules for the placement offshore Lake Erie wind-powered electrical generation facilities.

- **Providing education and outreach** on topics including coastal resources, Lake Erie and Great Lakes ecosystems. One of OCM's more recent endeavors is a collaborative education program with the ODNR Division of Wildlife-Old Woman Creek National Estuarine Research Reserve, the Ohio Lake Erie Commission and the Ohio Sea Grant College Program. To aid in Lake Erie-related education, together we have developed *Lake Erie Literacy Principles and Concepts* which outline basic information people should know about Ohio's shared fresh water resource. The goal is to provide people an easy way to understand Lake Erie and be able to take personal actions that create a healthier lake and watershed. **Learn more:** ohiodnr.com/LakeErieLiteracy

- **Administering grants to improve the coastal area.** The OCMP has awarded more than $33.4 million in grants since the program was federally approved in 1997. Grants issued range from land acquisition from willing sellers to construction, planning, hazard mitigation and enhancing public access. Grants awarded to public access sites along Ohio's coast are mentioned in the site descriptions. Details about all grants awarded by the OCMP are found on the OCM website by selecting "Grants" in the top navigation.

- **With our partners, promoting effective management, protection and restoration of Ohio's coastal resources.** OCM coordinates with and seeks support from agencies and groups at the local, state and federal levels as well as internationally. Efforts include extensive mapping of the Lake Erie Watershed, land-use planning, erosion management planning, and coordination of groups working to improve Lake Erie and the watershed.

* *Lake Erie Region Tourism Economic Impact Study, Tourism Economics* through Ohio Department of Development, 2008.
** *Economic Impact of Great Lakes Fishing by State in 2006* (revised in 2008) by the American Sportfishing Association.

Beach Safety Tips

Throughout Lake Erie there is an interconnected circulation system powered by wind, waves, the sun, river flow and water density differences. The shape of Lake Erie's lakebed, its shore and the human-made structures along the shore influence the path of circulation.

Winds blowing across Erie's 127.7 trillion gallons of water create waves. When the waves interact with the lakebed, shore and human-made structures, various phenomena may occur which do not happen on inland lakes or in swimming pools. By making oneself aware of these conditions and what to do in an emergency, one can help ensure they explore the shore safely.

Rip currents

Due to lakebed variations, waves may break strongly in some locations and weakly in others causing the water to converge in narrow, river-like currents moving away from shore. These are known as rip currents and can occur at any beach with breaking waves.

Rip currents do not pull people under the water; they pull people away from shore. The size and lakeward pull of rip currents varies. Drowning usually occurs when people panic and are unable to keep themselves afloat.

Signs of rip currents can include a channel of churning, choppy water; an area of water of a different color; a line of algae or debris moving steadily offshore; or a break in the incoming wave pattern (waves usually do not break as readily in a rip current as in adjacent water).

Rip currents are more likely to form near beaches with a sand bar and channel system in the near shore. They can also occur when a water current traveling along the shore is interrupted by a structure such as a groin or jetty. Extra precaution should be taken when swimming near shore structures.

If caught in a rip current, you will feel yourself being pulled away from the shore. The National Oceanic and Atmospheric Administration recommends taking the following actions:

- Remain calm to conserve energy and think clearly.

- Never fight the current. Instead, swim out of the current in a direction parallel to the shore or float/tread water until the current stops pulling you lakeward.

- When out of the current, swim at an angle away from the current toward the shore.
- If you are still unable to reach shore, draw attention to yourself by waving your arm and yelling for help.

If you see someone in trouble, get help from a lifeguard, or call 9-1-1; throw the victim something that floats and yell instructions on how to escape.

SwimSafe! and *Wear It Ohio!* **Beach safety tips:**

- Swim only in designated areas.
- Encourage children and those who are not strong swimmers to wear life jackets - especially while swimming during high wave action.
- Designate one person to remain on the beach to watch those who are swimming.
- Exercise caution since lakes may have unseen drop-offs in the lakebed.
- Take a cell phone to make an emergency call if necessary.
- Be aware of heavy wave action and strong currents.

Lake Erie Boating

Registrations are required for every recreational boat in Ohio, including canoes, kayaks, pedal and inflated boats. Boats can be registered online or at an ODNR Division of Watercraft office.

People born on or after January 1, 1982, who operate a boat on Ohio water that is powered by greater than a 10 horsepower engine, must successfully pass a NASBLA-approved (National Association of State Boating Law Administrators) boating education course or proficiency exam.

Ohio law requires life jackets to be worn while riding a personal watercraft, while waterskiing or while being towed on a similar device, and by children less than 10 years of age on any vessel less than 18-feet long. Additionally, it is particularly important to wear a life jacket when the boater cannot swim or is a weak swimmer; when boating alone; when the water is dangerously cold (October through May in Ohio); during rough water/waves and severe weather conditions; when boating at night; in emergency situations and in swift and fast currents.

Learn more: ohiodnr.com/watercraft

Bathing Beach Water Quality Monitoring

The water quality at some public beaches along Lake Erie is seasonally sampled for E. coli bacteria in accordance with the Ohio Department of Health's (ODH) bathing Beach Monitoring Program. The presence of E. coli bacteria in the nearshore water is an indicator of pollution that could be potentially harmful to swimmers – especially those with weakened immune systems. When the amount of bacteria in the water exceeds 235 E. coli colony forming units (cfu) per 100mL of water sampled, signs are posted advising against swimming.

The ODH maintains Webpages dedicated to Ohio's Beach Monitoring Program with sampling results from the current and archived years. Some Ohio coastal counties also have testing programs and/or permitting programs for bathing beaches. Those programs include the Erie County Health Department (25 public and nonpublic sites), the city of Lorain Health Department, the Cuyahoga County Board of Health (24 public and nonpublic sites including Ohio Nowcast sites (www.ohionowcast.info/index.asp), the Lake County General Health District and the Ashtabula County Health Department.

Learn more: Ohio Department of Health Beach Monitoring Program
www.odh.ohio.gov/odhPrograms/eh/bbeach/beachmon.aspx

Ohio Water Trails

Recognizing the rising popularity of canoeing and kayaking, various ODNR divisions collaborated to initiate the Ohio Water Trails Program. The program helps address the need for increased paddling access points and helps educate paddlers about hand-powered boating safety on Ohio's waterways. Over the past few years, the Ohio Water Trails program has evolved into a cooperative partnership between ODNR, various levels of government and non-profit conservation groups. The program promotes paddling routes that combine recreation with low-impact use. This is accomplished by designating waterways as State Water Trails and providing funding for site improvement and development; purchasing and installing access and hazard signage; and producing and distributing educational maps and brochures. As if March 2010, Ohio has designated the following water trails: the Kokosing Scenic River, the Muskingum River, the East Sandusky Bay, and the Vermilion-Lorain. Additional Ohio Water Trails are being planned that will improve access to Lake Erie and its tributaries.

Learn more: ohiodnr.com/tabid/2987/default.aspx

Clean Marinas

The Ohio Clean Marinas Program benefits the Lake Erie environment and economy. The program is a proactive partnership designed to encourage marinas and boaters to use simple, innovative solutions to keep Ohio's coastal and inland waterway resources clean. The program's goal is environmental stewardship by making marinas more aware of environmental laws and rules and to get marinas to follow best management practices and to be designated as a "Clean Marina." More than 40 of Ohio's coastal marinas (commercial and public) have made a commitment to follow voluntary practices that protect the coastal environment including clean water and fresh air.

Boat Shrink-Wrap Recycling Program

Since 2006, the Ohio Clean Marinas Program, together with Ohio company Mondo Polymer Technologies Inc., has recycled more than 1 million pounds of boat shrink-wrap. Marinas save an average of $500 annually in reduced waste disposal costs. The recycled material has produced nearly 150,000 guardrail blocks, enough to line almost 200 miles of Ohio highway.

Clean Boating

The Ohio Clean Boater Program is a proactive partnership designed to encourage marinas and boaters to use simple, innovative solutions to keep Ohio's coastal and inland waterway resources clean. The basic goal of the program is environmental stewardship by making marinas and boaters more aware of environmental laws, rules and jurisdictions, and to get as many boaters as possible to follow best boater practices and to be designated as "Clean Boaters."

Learn more:
www.ohiocleanmarina.osu.edu
www.ohioseagrant.osu.edu/cleanmarinas/shrinkwrap
www.ohioseagrant.osu.edu/cleanboaters

Lucas County

Lake Erie Public River Access

Boat Launch Sites and/or **Transient/Complimentary Dockage Sites** located along Lake Erie's tributaries or other lake accessible waterways within the designated Coastal Management Area. *Learn more about the designated Coastal Management Area at* ohiodnr.com/coastal/tabid/9352/default.aspx

L = Launch Only   D = Dock Only   L/D = Launch and Dock

Ottawa River
- President Drive Boat Launch in Washington Township - L
- Belpre Drive Boat Launch in Washington Township - L
- Hammond Drive Boat Launch in Washington Township - L

Maumee River
- Promenade Park in Toledo - L
- Walbridge Park in Toledo - L
- Toledo Skyway Marina in Toledo - D
- International Park in Toledo - L
- Corey Street Boat Launch in Maumee - L

Cooley Canal
- Cooley Canal Boat Launch in Jerusalem Township - L

Wood County

Maumee River
- Rossford Marina at Veteran's Memorial Park in Rossford - L
- Maple Street Boat Launch in Perrysburg - L
- Louisiana Avenue Dock at Hood Park in Perrysburg - D
- Orleans Park in Perrysburg - D

Ottawa County

Turtle Creek
- Turtle Creek Access in Benton Township - L

Toussaint River
- *No publicly accessible boat launch or dock site within Coastal Management Area*

Portage River
- Portage River Access in Erie Township - L
- Little Portage State Wildlife Area in Bay Township - L
- Port Clinton City Docks in Port Clinton - D

West Harbor
- West Harbor Public Boat Launch Ramp in Catawba Island Township - L

Sandusky County
Sandusky River
 Elliot Street Access in Fremont - L

Erie County
Huron River
 Huron Boat Basin and Amphitheatre in Huron - D
 Holiday Harbor Marina* in Huron - L
 Huron River Access in Huron - L
Vermilion River
 Harbour Town Municipal Boat Docks in Vermilion - D
 East Exchange Park in Vermilion - D
 McGarvey's Landing in Vermilion - D
 South Street Boat Ramp in Vermilion - L

Lorain County
Black River
 Black River Wharf Boat Launch in Lorain - L/D

Cuyahoga County
Rocky River
 Rocky River Reservation in Lakewood - L
 Lakewood Port Authority in Lakewood - D
Cuyahoga River
 No publicly accessible boat launch or dock site within Coastal Management Area

Lake County
Chagrin River
 Eastlake Port Authority in Eastlake - L
Grand River
 Robert "Buck" Benson Memorial Public Docks in Grand River - D
 Olive Street Transient Dock Access in Grand River - D
 Bucky Rutherford Memorial Park in Grand River - D
 Grand River Landing in Fairport Harbor - L

Ashtabula County
Ashtabula River
 Ashtabula Transient Docks in Ashtabula - D
 Ashtabula Recreation Unlimited (ARU)* in Ashtabula - L
Conneaut River
 No publicly accessible boat launch or dock site within Coastal Management Area

Erie County

Lorain County

08
12
35
36
37
38-39
09 34
10 32-33
07-16 31
17-18 30
11
19 29
03 06 22
02 05
04 23 24-28
20 21

Erie

10
09 13
08 12
05-06 07
03-04
01-02
11

Lorain

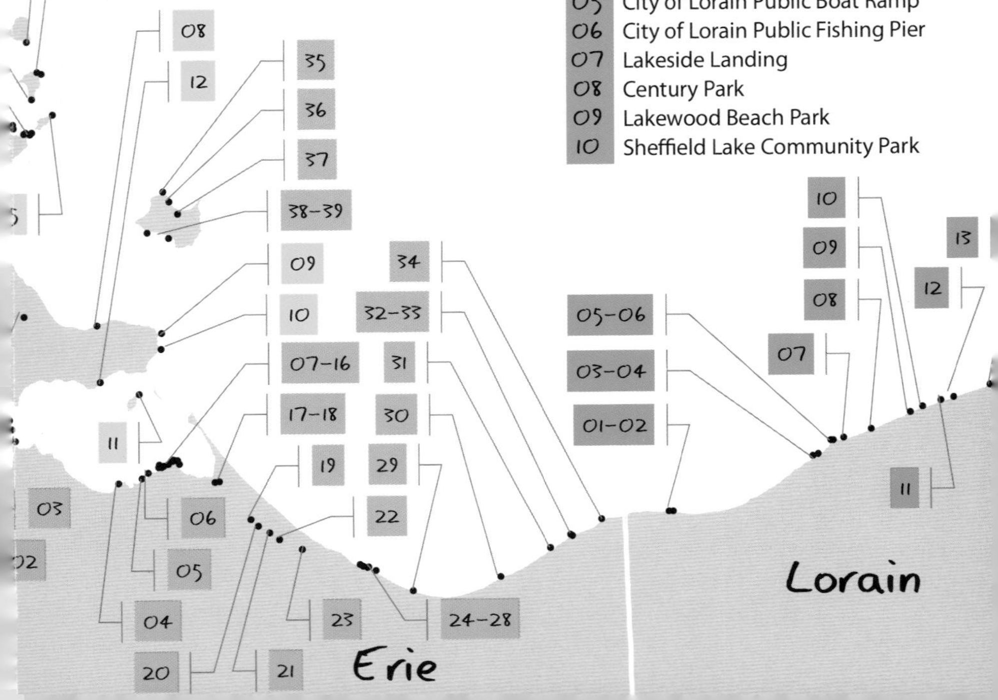

Lucas County

01	Cullen Park
02	Bayshore Fishing Access
03	Caldwell Drive Scenic Access
04	Duchesse Drive Scenic Access
05	South Shore Veterans Park
06	Lakeview Avenue Scenic Access
07	Verdun Street Scenic Access
08	Grange Street Scenic Access
09	Ashcroft Drive Basin Scenic Access
10	Blanche Drive Scenic Access
11	Lilias Drive Scenic Access
12	Lake Erie Center Basin Scenic Access
13	Maumee Bay State Park
14	Mallard Club Marsh State Wildlife Area
15	Metzger Marsh State Wildlife Area

Sandusky County

01	Pickerel Creek State Wildlife Area

Ottawa County

01	Magee Marsh State Wildlife Area
02	Camp Perry
03	Waterworks Park
04	Port Clinton Lakefront Preserve
05	Port Clinton City Beach
06	Catawba Island State Park
07	East Harbor State Park
08	Mazurik Access Area
09	Marblehead Lighthouse State Park
10	Lake Point Park
11	Johnson's Island Confederate Ceme
12	Dempsey's State Fishing Access
13	Sandusky Bay Bridge Access
14	South Bass Island Lighthouse
15	South Bass Island State Park
16	Captain Parker's Park
17	West Shore Ice Ramp - South
18	West Shore Ice Ramp - North
19	Put-in-Bay Aquatic Visitors Center
20	Peach Point Research Laboratory
21	Oak Point State Park

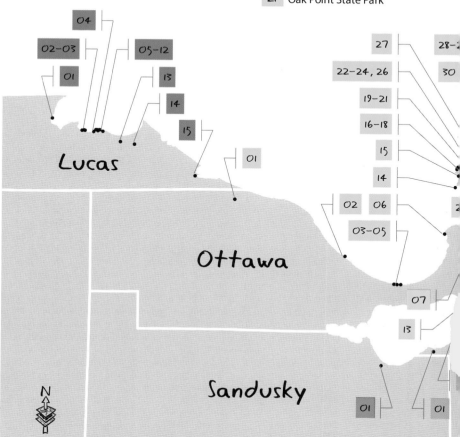

Fishing, Hunting and Trapping

Fishing opportunities abound on Lake Erie. The ODNR Division of Wildlife records Lake Erie fishing information weekly, and is available at: 1-888-HOOKFISH.

Fishing regulations including daily bag limits for sport fish caught in Ohio's Lake Erie waters are available by selecting "Fishing" and then "Fishing Regulations" on the Division of Wildlife's webpage: ohiodnr.com/wildlife.

Hunting and trapping regulations are also available on the Division of Wildlife's website by selecting "Hunting & Trapping" and then either "Hunting Regulations" or "Trapping Regulations." Local communities may also have regulations regarding where firearms may be discharged including required offshore distances.

Most Ohio residents and visitors who are older than 16 will need the appropriate fishing/hunting/trapping licenses, permits, and/or stamps to participate in the activity in Ohio; however, certain exemptions may apply. Details about exemptions and licenses are online or can be obtained by contacting the Division of Wildlife: 1-800-WILDLIFE.

For recipes on preparing fish and game visit the WildOhio Cookbook: ohiodnr.com/tabid/6470/default.aspx

To report fishing, hunting, trapping or other wildlife violation, call: 1-800-POACHER.

Fish Consumption

Fish consumption advisories have been issued for certain Lake Erie fish species and locations in Ohio. The ODNR Division of Wildlife and the Ohio Environmental Protection Agency (OEPA) work together to collect and analyze fish samples from Ohio's portion of Lake Erie. Results from the test samples dictate if restrictions are needed based on the Great Lakes risk assessment protocol for the consumption of fish by those most at risk (women of childbearing age and children). The general trend shows decreasing contamination levels over the last few decades. However, several locations and several fish species warrant special concern. Sport fish consumption advisories are periodically; the most recent updates found online.

Learn more:
Ohio Sport Fish Consumption Advisory – **Overall Advice**
epa.ohio.gov/dsw/fishadvisory/overall.aspx

Ohio Sport Fish Consumption Advisory for **Lake Erie**
epa.ohio.gov/dsw/fishadvisory/waters/Lakeerie.aspx

Lake Erie Coastal Ohio Trail

The Lake Erie Coastal Ohio Trail is a state and federally recognized path for vehicle traffic that primarily follows roads closest to Lake Erie from Toledo to Conneaut. The trail links harbors, lighthouses, natural wonders, historical attractions, tourist destinations and scenic views of Lake Erie.

The National Scenic Byways Program within the U.S. Department of Transportation designates roads as National Scenic Byways or All-American Roads based on their archaeological, cultural, historic, natural, recreational and scenic qualities. Spurred by grass-roots initiatives, 150 routes have been designated America's Byways® in 46 states. The Lake Erie Coastal Ohio Trail is one of only five nationally recognized Ohio byways. It was designated an Ohio State Scenic Byway in December 2004 and as a National Scenic Byway in the America's Byways® program in September 2005.

Learn more:
National Scenic Byways Program
www.byways.org/explore/byways/59836

Lake Erie Coastal Ohio Trail (Ohio)
www.dot.state.oh.us/OhioByways/Pages/LakeErieCoastalOhio.aspx

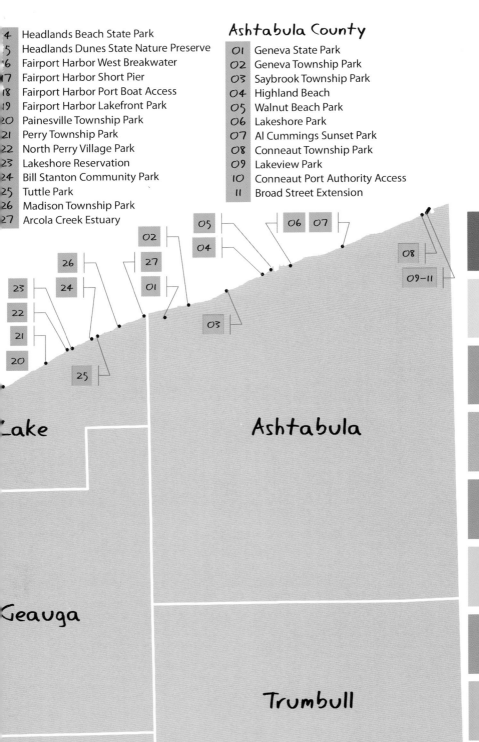

4 Headlands Beach State Park
5 Headlands Dunes State Nature Preserve
16 Fairport Harbor West Breakwater
17 Fairport Harbor Short Pier
18 Fairport Harbor Port Boat Access
19 Fairport Harbor Lakefront Park
20 Painesville Township Park
21 Perry Township Park
22 North Perry Village Park
23 Lakeshore Reservation
24 Bill Stanton Community Park
25 Tuttle Park
26 Madison Township Park
27 Arcola Creek Estuary

Ashtabula County

01 Geneva State Park
02 Geneva Township Park
03 Saybrook Township Park
04 Highland Beach
05 Walnut Beach Park
06 Lakeshore Park
07 Al Cummings Sunset Park
08 Conneaut Township Park
09 Lakeview Park
10 Conneaut Port Authority Access
11 Broad Street Extension

Lake

Ashtabula

Geauga

Trumbull

1 inch = 7 miles

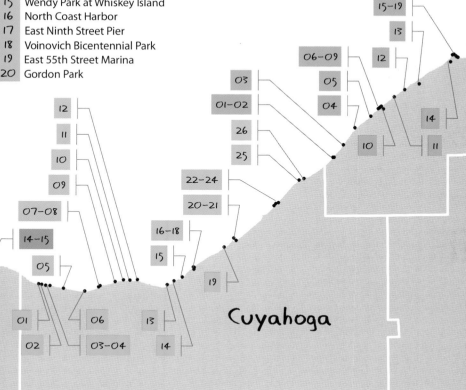

Ice on Lake Erie

Ohio's south shore sees ice fishing and across-ice snowmobiling, but there is no such thing as 100 percent safe ice. The following tips are useful for anyone who plays on water when it is frozen.

Check for known thin ice areas with a local resort, bait shop or professional ice fishing guide. Test the thickness of ice with a chisel, ice auger or even a cordless 1/4-inch drill with a long bit.

- 4 inches of new clear ice is the minimum thickness for travel on foot.
- 5 inches is minimum for snowmobiles and ATVs.
- 8 to 12 inches for cars or small trucks.

Refrain from driving on ice whenever possible. If you must drive a vehicle, be prepared to leave it in a hurry. Keep windows down, unbuckle your seat belt and have a simple emergency plan that you have discussed with your passengers. Do NOT wear a flotation device when traveling across the ice in an enclosed vehicle.

Do not "overdrive" your snowmobile's headlight. It can take a much longer distance to stop on ice than your headlight shines. Many snowmobile-through-ice accidents occur because the machine was traveling too fast for the operator to stop when the headlamp illuminated the hole in the ice. Wear a life vest under your winter gear, or wear one of a flotation suit designed for wearing on frozen lakes.

Carry a pair of ice picks to help pull yourself back onto the surface if you fall through.

Winter Activities

Lake Erie Public Access Site	Page	Sledding	Cross Country Skiing	Ice Fishing	Ice Skating	Ice Boating	Snowmobiling
East 55th Street Marina	238			*		*	
East Harbor State Park	60	*	*	*	*	*	*
Edgewater Park	228	*	*	*		*	
Euclid Beach Area	244			*		*	
Geneva State Park	302		*	*			*
Gordon Park	240			*		*	
Headlands Beach State Park	274	*	*				
Huntington Reservation	212	*	*	*			
Kelleys Island State Park	170		*	*	*		
Lakeview Park	186				*		
Maumee Bay State Park	40	*	*		*		
Metzger Marsh State Wildlife Area	45			*			
Pickerel Creek State Wildlife Area	101			*			
South Bass Island State Park	76			*	*		
South Shore Veterans Park	38	*					
Villa Angela Area	246			*		*	
Waterworks Park	52				*		
West Shore Ice Ramp – North	80			*		*	
West Shore Ice Ramp – South	80			*		*	
Wildwood Area	246			*		*	
Willow Point State Wildlife Area	104			*			

Established: June 20, 1835
2000 Population: 455,054
2010 Projection: 444,870
Land Area and Rank: 340.4 square miles, 85 of 88
County Seat: City of Toledo
Named for: Robert Lucas, Ohio Governor 1832-1836

Miles of Coast: 25 miles
Miles of Publicly Accessible Coast: 6.6 miles*
Number of Access Sites: 15

Lucas County

A brief history:

On August 20, 1794, near the present-day town of Maumee, American forces led by General Anthony Wayne won a decisive victory over combined American Indian forces at the Battle of Fallen Timbers. The battle opened the entire Northwest Territory for settlement.

Fearing its absorption into the Michigan territory, the Ohio General Assembly passed an act on June 20, 1835 to create Lucas County. Residents chose the name "Lucas" in honor of Robert Lucas, then governor of Ohio. In this same year, the legislature of the Michigan territory appropriated funds and put out a call for volunteers to prevent the present-day Toledo-area from being seized by Ohio. The "Toledo War," as this conflict became known, was settled by the U.S. Congress, which designated the disputed 400 square miles of land to Ohio on June 15, 1836. As restitution, Congress gave Michigan, when it became a state, 9,000 square miles of land now known as the Upper Peninsula. The water boundary between the two states continued to be disputed until the U.S. Supreme Court issued a decree on February 22, 1973, fixing the Ohio-Michigan boundary line in Lake Erie where it is today. The boundary divides Turtle Island, which is in Maumee Bay.

During the late nineteenth century, Toledo obtained its nickname "Glass City" for its numerous glass-producing facilities. The city was also the home of the Willys-Overland Company, the largest manufacturer of U.S. military personnel vehicles during World War II.

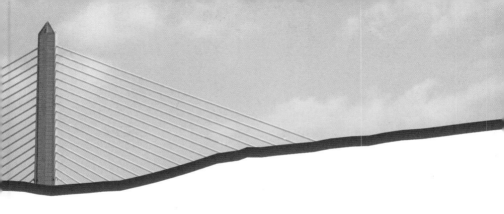

Learn More:

Lucas County
www.co.lucas.oh.us

City of Oregon
www.oregonohio.org

City of Toledo
www.ci.toledo.oh.us

Toledo Convention and Visitors Bureau
www.dotoledo.org

Toledo Region Chamber of Commerce
www.toledochamber.com

Eastern Maumee Bay Chamber of Commerce
www.embchamber.org

Jerusalem Township
www.twp.jerusalem.oh.us

Metroparks of the Toledo Area
www.metroparkstoledo.com

Public Access Management:

Local	11
State	4

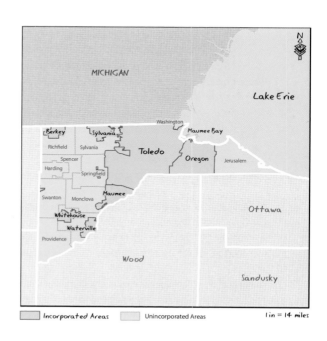

Incorporated Areas   Unincorporated Areas   1 in = 14 miles

Magee Marsh State Wildlife Area is inventoried as an Ottawa County access site, although a portion of it extends into Lucas County. Miles of publicly accessible shore at Magee Marsh (3.46 total miles) are broken down by county (2.02 miles in Ottawa County and 1.44 miles in Lucas County).

Cullen Park

Location:
Summit Street
near 101st Street
4526 Summit Street
Toledo, OH

Latitude:
N 41° 42.23'

Longitude:
W 083° 28.69'

Waterbody:
Maumee Bay

Access Site Type:
Recreational

Environments:
Manmade Shore
Sandy Beach

The 36-acre Cullen Park is Ohio's westernmost Lake Erie public access site and the city of Toledo's only site with direct access to Maumee Bay. It is also the only access location between the Ohio-Michigan state line and the Maumee River mouth. As noted on the entrance sign, Cullen Park is a public boat launch facility. The park also provides fishing access, trailer parking, benches affording scenic views, and the occasional lake freighter sighting.

Cullen Park's Point Place Path is a paved walking trail extending south between Summit Street and the bay and leading to a replica lighthouse and scenic area. The two-mile (round trip) Squadron Island Nature Trail is a dirt hiking path that traverses a seemingly natural, well-foliaged, but artificial pier. Seamlessly connected at the end of the manmade pier is Squadron Island, a natural island. Countless potential fishing sites can be accessed via the Squadron Island Nature Trail, as can many pocket beaches and bird viewing spots are located along its length.

The present location of Cullen Park is near the former site of Lake Erie Amusement Park and Casino, first built in 1895. The long-defunct amusement venue once featured rides, games, a boardwalk and vaudeville shows. Like many turn-of-the-Century amusement parks, fire spelled its downfall; the original pier burned in 1901 as did its replacement in 1910.

Field Notes:

_____

_____

_____

_____

_____

_____

Amenities and Services:

Location Map:

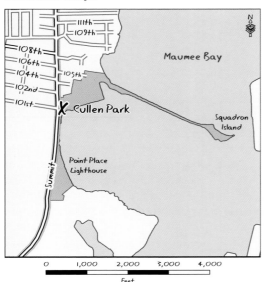

_____

_____

_____

_____

_____

_____

_____

_____

_____

_____

_____

_____

Date Visited: _____

Learn More:
City of Toledo
Division of Parks and Forestry
(419) 936-2873
www.ci.toledo.oh.us

Bayshore Fishing

Location:
Bayshore Road
West of Wynn Road
Oregon, OH

Latitude:
N 41° 41.41'

Longitude:
W 083° 25.87'

Waterbody:
Maumee Bay

**Access
Site Type:**
Outdoor
Wildlife

Environments:
Manmade Shore
Rocky Shore

Dedicated on July 1, 1999, the 8.2-acre Bayshore Fishing Access site in Oregon includes a single-lane boat ramp and short dock to fish from. The water is very shallow in the nearshore. Depending on the water level, a portion of the shore to the immediate east of the launch may have an exposed muddy-sand beach. The portion of the shore to the immediate west of the boat launch is covered by a stone revetment which provides fishing access for the surefooted.

The parking is designed to serve vehicles towing boat trailers and provides parking spaces for these and non-trailer vehicles. Handicapped accessible restrooms are on site.

An additional fishing hotspot, literally, is at Bayshore Fishing Access's easternmost side adjacent to the First Energy Corps. Bay Shore Power Plant's warm water discharge. To reach this prime fishing spot, visitors must walk a nearly 2,000-foot long (0.38 mile) trail. The trail extends west of the Bayshore Fishing Access parking lot and is sandwiched between the adjacent power plant's entryway and the shore. A sign on the west side of the parking lot marks the trailhead.

Access

Amenities and Services:

Location Map:

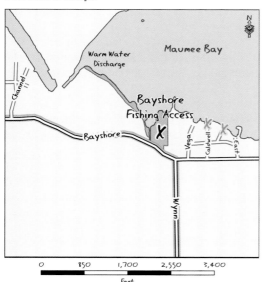

Field Notes:

_____ .

_____

_____

_____

_____

_____

_____

_____

_____

_____

_____

_____

_____

_____

_____

_____

_____

_____

_____

_____

_____

Date Visited: _____

Learn More:
ODNR Division of Wildlife
ohiodnr.com/wildlife

City of Oregon

Location:
Oregon, OH

Waterbody:
Maumee Bay

Access Site Type Basins:
Scenic

Access Site Type Rights-of-Way:
Right-of-Way
Scenic

Environments Basins:
Bluff
Sandy Beach

Environments Rights-of-Way:
Mixed

The city of Oregon maintains seven public road rights-of-way and two unimproved parkland basins that dead end or abut Maumee Bay. From west to east, the right-of-way sites include Caldwell and Duchesse drives, Lakeview Avenue, Verdun and Grange streets and Blanche and Lilias drives. The unimproved parklands (west to east) are the Ashcroft Drive and the Lake Erie Center basins. All nine sites are opportune for scenic vistas of Maumee Bay and fishing. None of the sites are marked with signs denoting public access other than a sign per site reading, "No Dumping. $250 Fine. 30 Days in Jail." The sites do not have designated parking areas. Visitors must park on the street where permissible.

The right-of-way sites offer no recreational amenities. The two basin locations both feature beaches comprised of natural sand and well-ground zebra and quagga mussel shell fragments. At all nine sites, people should be aware of the possibility of dumped concrete with exposed rebar lying just below surface waters.

A dirt path at Ashcroft Drive makes the beach easily reachable. Of these Oregon sites, the 4.5-acre Lake Erie Center basin, located across Bayshore Road from the University of Toledo's Lake Erie Center, provides the largest area of green space and is suitable for picnicking. The site has ample green space for common recreation activities such as throwing a Frisbee, baseball or football.

West

1 – Caldwell Drive Access
2 – Duchesse Drive Access

Maumee Bay

Bayshore
Fishing Access

Vega
Caldwell
East
Bayshore
Wynn

| 0 | 850 | 1,700 | 2,550 | 3,400 |

Feet

East

1 – Lakeview Avenue Access
2 – Verdun Street Access
3 – Grange Street Access
4 – Ashcroft Drive Basin Access
5 – Blanche Drive Access
6 – Lilias Drive Access
7 – Lake Erie Center Access

Maumee Bay

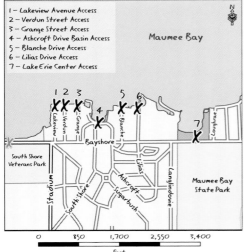

Lakeview
Verdun
Grange
Blanche
Loughrae
Bayshore
South Shore
Veterans Park
Stadium
South Shore
Lilias
Ashcroft
Sugarbush
Langlindove
Maumee Bay
State Park

| 0 | 850 | 1,700 | 2,550 | 3,400 |

Feet

Field Notes:

Date Visited: _____

Learn More:
City of Oregon
Streets Division
(419) 698-7046
www.oregonohio.org

City of Oregon

Location:
Oregon, OH

Waterbody:
Maumee Bay

**Access
Site Type
Basins:**
Scenic

**Access
Site Type
Rights-of-Way:**
Right-of-Way
Scenic

**Environments
Basins:**
Bluff
Sandy Beach

**Environments
Rights-of-Way:**
Mixed

Basins Access

Amenities and Services:

Ashcroft Drive Basin Access
Ashcroft Drive
Latitude: N 41° 41.41'
Longitude: W 083° 24.36'

Lake Erie Center Basin Access
Bayshore Road, east of Lagundovie Road
6225 Bayshore Road
Latitude: N 41° 41.36'
Longitude: W 083° 23.91'

Rights-of-Way Access

Amenities and Services:

Caldwell Drive Access
End of Caldwell Drive
Latitude: N 41° 41.44'
Longitude: W 083° 25.67'

Field Notes:

_____

_____

Duchesse Drive Access
End of Duchesse Drive
Latitude: N 41° 41.42'
Longitude: W 083° 25.60'

Lakeview Avenue Access
End of Lakeview Avenue
Latitude: N 41° 41.48'
Longitude: W 083° 24.56'

Verdun Street Access
End of Verdun Street
Latitude: N 41° 41.48'
Longitude: W 083° 24.52'

Grange Street Access
End of Grange Street
Latitude: N 41° 41.47'
Longitude: W 083° 24.46'

Blanche Drive Access
End of Blanche Drive
Latitude: N 41° 41.47'
Longitude: W 083° 24.26'

Lilias Drive Access
End of Lilias Drive
Latitude: N 41° 41.47'
Longitude: W 083° 24.18'

Date Visited: _____

Learn More:
City of Oregon
Streets Division
(419) 698-7046
www.oregonohio.org

South Shore Vet

Location:
Corner of Bayshore
and Stadium roads
5700 Bayshore Road
Oregon, OH

Latitude:
N 41° 41.34'

Longitude:
W 083° 24.77'

Waterbody:
Maumee Bay

**Access
Site Type:**
Recreational

Environments:
Manmade Shore

The 35.4-acre South Shore Veterans Park is located both north and south of Bayshore Road in Oregon. Many of the park's recreational amenities, including a picnic shelter, ball fields, playground, basketball court, open space, exercise trail and an observation/sledding hill overlooking Lake Erie are on the south side of the road.

The north side of the park features a paved and lighted concrete, handicapped accessible walkway with benches overlooking Maumee Bay. The 600-foot boardwalk is armored with large limestone boulders and provides fishing access. In November 2001, the walkway was rededicated and named the James A. Haley Boardwalk, in honor of his public service to the citizens of the city for more than a quarter century.

South Shore Veterans Park is a convergence point for two bike trails that follow Bayshore and Stadium roads. The routes are components in an extensive network of biking trails that, when complete, will link the Maumee River to the west of Oregon to Maumee Bay State Park on the city's east-end. Many side-route bikeways are found along the way.

The James "Wes" Hancock Oregon Senior Center is also located at South Shore Veterans Park. The center is a gathering place for local seniors offering various recreation, nutrition, education and social programs along with volunteer opportunities.

rans Park

Amenities and Services:

Location Map:

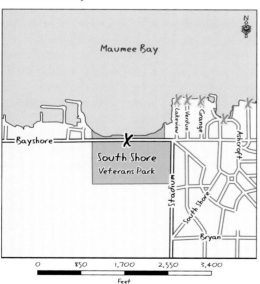

Maumee Bay

Bayshore

South Shore Veterans Park

Lakeview · Verdun · Grange · Ashcroft · Stadium · South Shore · Bryan

| 0 | 850 | 1,700 | 2,550 | 3,400 |

Feet

Field Notes:

Date Visited: _____

Learn More:
City of Oregon
Parks and Recreation Department
(419) 698-7146
www.oregonohio.org

Maumee Bay Sto

Location:
Cedar Point Road at
North Curtice Road
1400 State Park Road
City of Oregon and
Jerusalem Township, OH

Latitude:
N 41° 40.66'

Longitude:
W 083° 22.22'

Waterbody:
Maumee Bay

**Access
Site Type:**
Recreational

Environments:
Manmade Shore
Sandy Beach
Wetland

The 1,336-acre Maumee Bay State Park is the western-most state park on Ohio's Lake Erie shore. The park offers a multitude of amenities for day-use and overnight visitors including two beaches—a large beach on the bay and an inland lake swimming beach. The inland lake is also suitable for sailing and canoeing. Kayak rentals are available on the bay during summer months. The ODNR Division of Watercraft's Maumee Bay field office is located at the state park headquarters building. A 32-slip marina accessible from the bay is available to boaters by reservation.

The park is situated among scenic meadows, and marshlands and wetlands that are remnants of the Great Black Swamp. The park provides habitat to many animal and avian species. More than 300 types of birds have been recorded in the park. The park is also home to the Trautman Nature Center which is staffed year-round by a naturalist. The center features interactive displays, an auditorium, viewing windows and a research laboratory. Maumee Bay State Park includes an amphitheatre, Scottish Links-style golf course, a butterfly house and a 10-mile network of trails, including a bridle trail.

Overnight visitors can stay at the Maumee Bay Resort Lodge, in the deluxe cottages or at the 256-site campground. Use of some of the park's amenities, such as the lodge's swimming pools, is limited to lodgers and cottage guests.

e Park

Field Notes:

Amenities and Services:

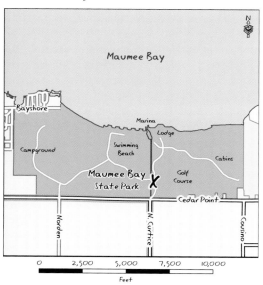

Location Map:

Maumee Bay

Bayshore

Marina

Lodge

Campground

Swimming Beach

Cabins

Maumee Bay State Park X

Golf Course

Cedar Point

Norden

N. Curtice

Cousino

| 0 | 2,500 | 5,000 | 7,500 | 10,000 |

Feet

Date Visited: _____

Learn More:
ODNR Division of Parks and Recreation
Maumee Bay State Park
(419) 836-7758
ohiodnr.com/parks
ohiodnr.com/tabid/764/default.aspx

Mallard Club Marsh

Location:
Cedar Point and
Decant roads
8763 Cedar Point Road
Jerusalem Township, OH

Latitude:
N 41° 40.51'

Longitude:
W 083° 20.87'

Waterbody:
Maumee Bay

**Access
Site Type:**
Outdoor
Wildlife

Environments:
Manmade Shore
Wetland

The 402-acre Mallard Club Marsh State Wildlife Area is geared for hunting, fishing and trapping. The area is sectioned into six marshlands separated by dikes and managed to provide wetland vegetation that sustains a variety of wildlife. The marsh has a pocket of wooded land on the property's western extent. The wildlife area is bounded to the west by Maumee Bay State Park and to the east and northeast by Cedar Point National Wildlife Refuge. A small portion of the marsh touches Maumee Bay.

The northern portion of Mallard Club Marsh was originally a private duck hunting club for which it is named. In 1974, the area was purchased by ODNR and in 1992 acquired by the Division of Wildlife. In 1994, cropland areas were rehabilitated to a wetland environment through dike renovation, installation of pumps and development of water supply channels for water level management.

Dirt and grass trails atop the dikes lead to prime hunting, fishing and wildlife viewing sites. More than 300 bird species frequent the area including waterfowl such as mallards, black ducks, wood ducks, and blue- and green-winged teal, and bald eagles, shorebirds and songbirds. Waterfowl hunting is popular during established seasons. Trapping is permitted; muskrats, raccoon and mink are common.

Mallard Club Marsh State Wildlife Area has three gravel parking lots along Cedar Point Road.

tate Wildlife Area

Amenities and Services:

Field Notes:

_____

_____

_____

_____

Location Map:

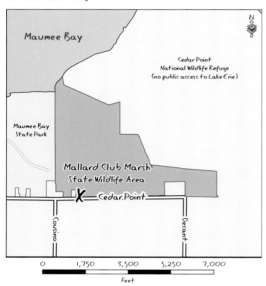

Date Visited: _____

Learn More:
ODNR Division of Wildlife
ohiodnr.com/wildlife
ohiodnr.com/tabid/19779/default.aspx

Metzger Marsh S†

Location:
Bono Road off
State Route 2
12600 Bono Road
Jerusalem Township, OH

Latitude:
N 41° 38.33'

Longitude:
W 083° 15.07'

Waterbody:
Lake Erie

**Access
Site Type:**
Outdoor
Wildlife

Environments:
Manmade Shore
Riparian/River
Sandy Beach
Wetland

The 558-acre Metzger Marsh State Wildlife Area is in Jerusalem Township on Bono Road 13 miles east of Toledo.

Metzger Marsh is a remnant of the former Great Black Swamp which bordered most of western Lake Erie. The swamp was drained in the 1850s to aid transportation and agriculture. Today, only 15,000 acres of the swamp remain, many of which are preserved by Metzger and Magee state wildlife area marshes and the Ottawa National Wildlife Refuge complex.

Metzger Marsh's history includes being farmed and home to a duck club until it was purchased by the ODNR Division of Wildlife in 1955. The dike has been restored. Today, about 70 percent of the marsh consists of open water ranging from one to four feet; water levels are managed to provide optimum vegetation for wetland wildlife.

Birding, waterfowl hunting, trapping and fishing are the main uses of this site. A launch ramp connected to Wards Canal provides boaters with protected lake access. The boat launch and a small parking lot are south of Wards Canal and parallel to an access road on the wildlife area's east side. At the access road's northern terminus, a steel and concrete handicap-accessible fishing pier extends into Lake Erie. Parking and portable restrooms are available here. The site also provides ice anglers Lake Erie access.

A dirt trail running east from the pier parallel to the shore leads to a small pocket beach. The trail affords views of the surrounding marshes and Lake Erie.

...te Wildlife Area

Amenities and Services:

Location Map:

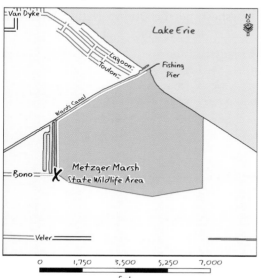

Van Dyke

Lake Erie

Lagoon
Toulon

Fishing Pier

Wards Canal

Bono

X Metzger Marsh
State Wildlife Area

Veler

0   1,750   3,500   5,250   7,000
Feet

N

Field Notes:

_____
_____
_____
_____
_____
_____
_____
_____
_____
_____
_____
_____
_____
_____
_____

Date Visited: _____

Learn More:
ODNR Division of Wildlife
ohiodnr.com/wildlife
ohiodnr.com/tabid/19782/default.aspx

Established: March 6, 1840
2000 Population: 40,985
2010 Projection: 40,800
Land Area and Rank: 255.1 square miles, 86 of 88
County Seat: City of Port Clinton
Named for: Native American word meaning "trader"

Miles of Coast: 94 miles
Miles of Publicly Accessible Coast: 14.4 miles*
Number of Access Sites: 30

Ottawa County

A brief history:

On March 6, 1840, Ottawa County was created out of 225-square miles of land – a majority of which was part of the Great Black Swamp. Residents took the Native American word for "trader" as the county's name.

Ottawa County was originally part of territory set aside for Ohio's Native American people by the Treaty of Greenville. During the War of 1812, the Battle of Lake Erie occurred off the coast in waters near the present-day Bass islands. At that time, the islands of South Bass, Middle Bass and North Bass were named Bass Island, Isle des Fleures and Isle St. George, respectively. The county's Johnson's Island served as a prisoner of war camp during the American Civil War. The county is also home of Camp Perry, an Ohio National Guard training base.

The county includes seven villages and twelve townships.

Ottawa County is 95 percent rural and five percent urban. The county is a major tourist destination with visitors pursuing boating, fishing, visiting the Lake Erie Islands and other recreational activities. Located at the eastern tip of the Marblehead peninsula, the Marblehead Lighthouse is the oldest lighthouse in Ohio and is the oldest continually operating lighthouse on the Great Lakes.

*Magee Marsh State Wildlife Area is inventoried as an Ottawa County access site, although a portion of it extends into Lucas County. Miles of publicly accessible shore at Magee Marsh (3.46 total miles) are broken down by county (2.02 miles in Ottawa County and 1.44 miles in Lucas County).

Learn More:

Ottawa County
www.co.ottawa.oh.us

Catawba Island Township
catawbaislandtownship.com

Carroll Township
carrolltownship.net

City of Port Clinton
www.ci.port-clinton.oh.us

Danbury Township
danburytownship.com

Lake Erie Shores & Islands (West)
shoresandislands.com

Lakeside
lakesideohio.com

Marblehead Peninsula Chamber of Commerce
marbleheadpeninsula.com

Port Clinton Chamber of Commerce
portclintonchamber.com

Put-in-Bay Chamber of Commerce/Visitors Bureau
visitputinbay.com

Put-in-Bay Township
www.pibtownship.com

Village of Marblehead
marbleheadvillageohio.com

Public Access Management:

State	14
Local	11
Federal	4
Non-Profit	1

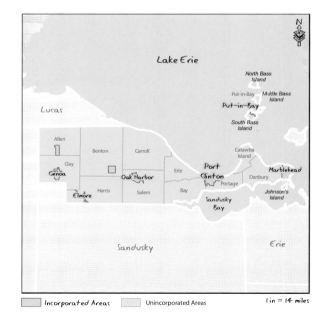

Magee Marsh Sta

Location:
State Route 2 at
Benton-Carroll Road
13229 West
State Route 2
Carroll Township
(Ottawa County)
Jerusalem Township
(Lucas County)

Latitude:
N 41° 36.72′

Longitude:
W 083° 11.32′

Waterbody:
Lake Erie

**Access
Site Type:**
Outdoor
Wildlife

Environments:
Riparian/River
Sandy Beach
Wetland

The 2,202-acre Magee Marsh State Wildlife Area encompasses some of Ohio's finest remaining wetlands. Historically, the marsh was part of the Great Black Swamp. Today, Magee is a haven for bald eagles, great blue herons, egrets, kestrel, tundra swans and other avian and terrestrial non-game and game species.

The main entrance is off State Route 2 in Ottawa County; the area straddles Lucas and Ottawa counties. The entrance leads to the Sportsmen's Migratory Bird Center, trails and wildlife beach. Magee Marsh's Turtle Creek Access drive is located about 1.5 miles east of the main entrance and hosts a small boat launch and fishing access. Magee Marsh offers seasonal controlled hunting.

The Sportsmen's Migratory Bird Center features exhibits on the history of the marsh and an extensive collection of mounted birds and mammals that inhabit the marsh. The center is surrounded by a display pond, walking trail and 42-foot tall observation deck that offers views of the marshes and Lake Erie. Additional trails include the Wildlife Beach Trail, the Bird Trail and the Magee/Ottawa Partnership Trail, which connects to the adjacent Ottawa National Wildlife Refuge.

In 2008, the management of Crane Creek State Park beach and picnic area was transferred to the ODNR Division of Wildlife. While the site is no longer a swimming beach, it is accessible for fishing and wildlife viewing.

e Wildlife Area

Amenities and Services:

Field Notes:

_____

_____

_____

_____

Location Map:

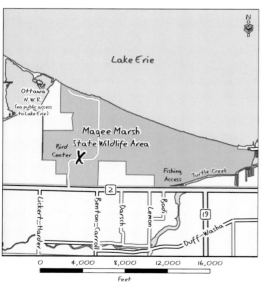

Lake Erie

Ottawa N.W.R. (no public access to Lake Erie)

Magee Marsh State Wildlife Area

Bird Center X

Fishing Access

Turtle Creek

2

Lickert-Harder

Benton-Carroll

Darsch

Lemon

Bodi

19

Duff-Washa

0   4,000   8,000   12,000   16,000

Feet

_____

_____

_____

_____

_____

_____

_____

_____

_____

_____

_____

_____

_____

_____

Date Visited: _____

Learn More:
ODNR Division of Wildlife
Magee Marsh State Wildlife Area
(419) 898-0960
ohiodnr.com/wildlife
ohiodnr.com/tabid/19778/default.aspx

Camp Perry

Location:
Lawrence and
Scorpion roads
1000 Lawrence Road
Erie Township, OH

Latitude:
N 41° 32.79′

Longitude:
W 083° 00.81′

Waterbody:
Lake Erie

**Access
Site Type:**
Cultural
Recreational

Environments:
Sandy Beach

The 640-acre Camp Perry Military Reservation is an Ohio National Guard Training Site for the Air National Guard's 200th Red Horse Squadron and home to the NRA National Outdoor Rifle & Pistol Championships.

Camp Perry was selected as a military training site by an Ohio general during his 1905 hunting trip to area marshes. In September 1907, the first National Rifle Matches were hosted. By 1909, Camp Perry had evolved into one of the best equipped rifle and pistol ranges in the world. Over the years, Camp Perry has played a role in various wars and military efforts including both World Wars. The camp is named for Commodore Oliver Hazard Perry, the American Commander who defeated the British naval forces in 1813 in the Battle of Lake Erie.

Today, the annual national shooting matches are held for five weeks in July and August, attracting premier shooters from around the world. Spectators are welcome. The camp also serves local and federal law enforcement agencies, weekend range firing, civilian rifle teams and non-military agencies.

Available for public use, Camp Perry offers a swimming beach, fishing pier and restroom located near the Camp Perry Lodging & Conference Center facility on Lawrence Road. Camp Perry also boasts a museum, conference center, and self-guided tours by following signs posted throughout. Lodging, conference and banquet facilities are available for rent.

Camp Perry's main entrance, Niagara Road, is the northern continuation of State Route 358 north of State Route 2. Photo identification is required at the gate to enter.

Amenities and Services:

      P

 ID

Location Map:

Field Notes:

Date Visited: _____

Learn More:
Ohio National Guard
Camp Perry
www.cplcc.com

Waterworks Park

Location:
East Perry Street (SR 163) at Jefferson Street Port Clinton, OH

Latitude:
N 41° 30.86'

Longitude:
W 082° 56.13'

Waterbody:
Lake Erie
Portage River

Access Site Type:
Recreational

Environments:
Riparian/River
Wetland

Waterworks Park in downtown Port Clinton borders Lake Erie and the Portage River. Fishing access is available along the river and from the Jefferson Street Pier that extends into the lake at the river's mouth. A dense buffer of vegetation along the lakeshore makes direct water access difficult. The park does not have a swimming beach; however Port Clinton City Beach is located to the east. The Port Clinton Lakefront Preserve, acquired by the city in November 2009, creates a seamless stretch of publicly accessible shore connecting Waterworks Park to the city beach.

In addition to the paved walkway along the river, Waterworks Park has a handicap accessible paved walking trail, funded in part by an Ohio Coastal Management Program grant. The trail meanders through the park and along the shore terminating at the east end of the property north of Derby Pond. Other amenities include picnic facilities, playground equipment, a skate park, baseball field and Derby Pond which is stocked for children's fishing enjoyment.

A limited-time free parking lot is located north of Perry Street (State Route 163) at Jefferson Street. The Jefferson Street Pier offers a parking lot which at times includes a gate fee. Additional free parking is found south of Perry Street along Adams Street and throughout the downtown area.

Field Notes:

Amenities and Services:

Location Map:

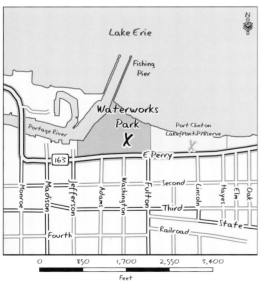

Date Visited: _____

Learn More:
City of Port Clinton
(419) 734-5522
www.portclinton.com

Port Clinton Lal

Location:
East Perry Street
(SR 163) and
Lincoln Street
Port Clinton, OH

Latitude:
N 41° 30.85'

Longitude:
W 082° 55.85'

Waterbody:
Lake Erie

**Access
Site Type:**
Natural

Environments:
Sandy Beach
Wetland

One of the most recent public acquisitions along Ohio's coast, the Port Clinton Lakefront Preserve connects two existing parks to create a nearly one mile stretch of Lake Erie access.

In November 2009 the city of Port Clinton finalized the purchase of the preserve, which includes 12 acres of coastal wetlands, marsh and a one-third mile sand beach.

The acquisition preserves waterfowl and bird habitat and connects the city's Waterworks Park on the west to Port Clinton City Beach on the east.

The preserve is located north of East Perry Street (State Route 163). The road is part of the Lake Erie Coastal Ohio Trail of the National Scenic Byways Program; the land, part of the Atlantic and Mississippi flyways for migratory birds, is an Audubon Ohio designated Important Bird Area.

The land was purchased with funding from the Coastal and Estuarine Land Conservation Program (CELCP) administered by the ODNR Office of Coastal Management, and a Clean Ohio Green Space Conservation Fund grant.

The city of Port Clinton, the Trust for Public Land and the Black Swamp Conservancy were integral partners in the land acquisition. The city of Port Clinton owns the property and Black Swamp Conservancy holds a conservation easement over the preserve, requiring that the land be permanently maintained as a nature preserve.

efront Preserve

Amenities and Services:

Location Map:

Lake Erie

Fishing Pier

Port Clinton
Lakefront Preserve

Portage River

Waterworks Park

Port Clinton City Beach

163

E. Perry

Lakeview City Park

Jefferson

Adams

Washington

Fulton

Second

Lincoln

Hayes

Elm

Oak

Ash

Beech

Cedar

Walnut

Linden

Third

State

Fourth

Railroad

| 0 | 850 | 1,700 | 2,550 | 3,400 |

Feet

Field Notes:

_____

_____

_____

_____

_____

_____

_____

_____

_____

_____

_____

_____

_____

_____

_____

_____

Date Visited: _____

Learn More:
City of Port Clinton
(419) 734-5522
www.portclinton.com

Port Clinton City

Location:
East Perry Street
(SR 163)
Port Clinton, OH

Latitude:
N 41° 30.84′

Longitude:
W 082° 55.49′

Waterbody:
Lake Erie

**Access
Site Type:**
Recreational

Environments:
Sandy Beach

Port Clinton City Beach is located on the north side of East Perry Street (State Route 163) between Hayes and Maple streets. The 2,180-foot long beach is a popular swimming location. Residents and visitors enjoy relaxing and playing on the foot-friendly sand which is mixed with shells and shell fragments near the water's edge.

A few permanent benches and a brick wall which serves as a sand barrier are located north of East Perry Street. Other available amenities are located on the south side of the street at Lakeview City Park.

Lakeview City Park's recreational facilities, including parking for the park and beach, are located in the park on the south side of the road. Park amenities include a picnic shelter, playgrounds, restrooms and basketball court. A crosswalk with a pedestrian-activated traffic signal allows the public to safely cross the road from the park to the beach during high-traffic summer months.

Adjacent to the west of the city beach is the newly acquired Port Clinton Lakefront Preserve. Waterworks Park is adjacent to and west of the preserve. Ongoing improvements at these three sites were outlined in the city of Port Clinton's *2000 Comprehensive Coastal Land Area Master Plan* which was funded in part by a grant from the Ohio Coastal Management Program.

Beach

Amenities and Services:

Location Map:

Field Notes:

_____

_____

_____

_____

_____

_____

_____

_____

_____

_____

_____

_____

_____

_____

_____

_____

_____

_____

Date Visited: _____

Ottawa County

Learn More:
City of Port Clinton
(419) 734-5522
www.portclinton.com

Catawba Island

Location:
End of East Moore's
Dock Road, west of
NW Catawba Road
4049 East Moore's
Dock Road
Catawba Island
Township, OH

Latitude:
N 41° 34.45'

Longitude:
W 082° 51.41'

Waterbody:
Lake Erie

**Access
Site Type:**
Recreational

Environments:
Rocky Shore
Manmade Shore

The nearly 10-acre Catawba Island State Park is a day-use park primarily used for Lake Erie fishing access. The park is located on the west side of the Catawba Island peninsula on East Moore's Dock Road which is west off of NW Catawba Road.

The park features a large fishing pier, a three-lane public boat ramp, 120 car-trailer parking slips and car-only parking, picnic and restroom facilities, and a playground. A 400-foot smooth cobble beach stretches northwest from the fishing pier. The beach has an increasing amount of white sand from finely crushed zebra and quagga mussel shells. Swimming is permitted at one's own risk.

A historic boundary marker denoting the northwest corner of the Connecticut Western Reserve is on site. The Connecticut Western Reserve was an area of the Northwest Territory stretching from the current Ohio-Pennsylvania border west to the modern-day western boundary of Huron and Erie counties and extending north into Ottawa County. The state of Connecticut owned the Western Reserve, selling and distributing the land after the Revolutionary War.

State Park

Amenities and Services:

Location Map:

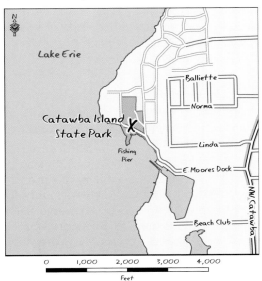

Lake Erie

Balliette

Norma

Catawba Island State Park X

Fishing Pier

Linda

E Moores Dock

NW Catawba

Beach Club

| 0 | 1,000 | 2,000 | 3,000 | 4,000 |

Feet

Field Notes:

_____

_____

_____

_____

_____

_____

_____

_____

_____

_____

_____

_____

_____

_____

_____

_____

Date Visited: _____

Learn More:
ODNR Division of Parks and Recreation
Catawba Island State Park
(419) 797-4530
ohiodnr.com/parks
ohiodnr.com/tabid/753/default.aspx

East Harbor Sta

Ottawa County

Location:
State Route 269
(Buck Road)
1169 North Buck Rd
Danbury Township, OH

Latitude:
N 41° 32.71'

Longitude:
W 082° 49.05'

Waterbody:
Lake Erie

Access Site Type:
Recreational

Environments:
Riparian/River
Rocky Shore
Sandy Beach
Manmade Shore
Wetland

East Harbor State Park features a range of natural settings and recreational opportunities to explore the outdoors. The park's nearly 2.25 mile Lake Erie shore includes a 1,500-foot swimming beach with fine natural sand. Four off-shore breakwaters slow Lake Erie waves and have made the designated swimming area very shallow. One of the park's 14 picnic areas is at the beach.

The park's 1,831 land acres have 10 miles of intertwining paved and dirt trails. The 11 trails range from a half mile to 2.5 miles. A paved multi-purpose trail also parallels the length of the park's main road.

Scenic wetlands and wildlife can be viewed throughout the park, including from various observation decks and viewing binoculars. Fishing is allowed on Lake Erie and within East and West harbors. Seasonal waterfowl hunting is permitted offshore east of the detached breakwaters.

The park's campground features 571-sites plus two deluxe camper cabins, two Rent-A-RV sites and 10 group camp sites, a store and a nature center. There are two boat ramps in the park – a free ramp for campers in the campground and a fee-ramp at the park's marina. The marina also offers seasonal and day-use dock rentals, fuel, a full-time mechanic and boat supplies. Winter activities at the park include cross-country skiing, ice skating (on Lake Erie and in the harbors), ice fishing, sledding and snowmobiling.

This state park has received various grants from the Ohio Coastal Management Program for planning and implementing improvements to the beach and access trails.

e Park

Amenities and Services:

Location Map:

West Harbor

Marina

Middle Harbor
Game Sanctuary

Buck

Lake Erie

Swimming
Beach

East Harbor
State Park

X

Campground

East Harbor

269

163

N

0   2,500   5,000   7,500   10,000

Feet

Field Notes:

_____

_____

_____

_____

_____

_____

_____

_____

_____

_____

_____

_____

_____

_____

_____

_____

Date Visited: _____

Learn More:
ODNR Division of Parks and Recreation
East Harbor State Park
(419) 734-4424
ohiodnr.com/parks
ohiodnr.com/tabid/733/default.aspx

Mazurik State A

Ottawa
County

Location:
North Shore Road at
Rockport Drive
8957 North Shore Rd
Danbury Township, OH

Latitude:
N 41° 32.46'

Longitude:
W 082° 45.81'

Waterbody:
Lake Erie

**Access
Site Type:**
Outdoor
Wildlife

Environments:
Manmade Shore
Rocky Shore

The 15.9-acre Mazurik Access Area is located on the north side of Marblehead Peninsula just west of Lakeside. This site provides boaters and anglers direct access to Lake Erie by offering a four-lane concrete boat ramp, a protected boat bay/safe harbor, and a handicap-accessible fishing pier. Smallmouth bass, walleye, white bass and yellow perch are common fish species caught at Mazurik and in Lake Erie.

By boat, Mazurik Access is just 7-miles south of South Bass Island. The access parking area has 215 car-and-trailer spaces and 40 car-only spaces. The lot is paved and lighted and accessible 24 hours a day. Other amenities at this access area are limited, but include restrooms, a paved trail and a small beach composed of large cobble and shell fragments.

ccess Area

Amenities and Services:

Location Map:

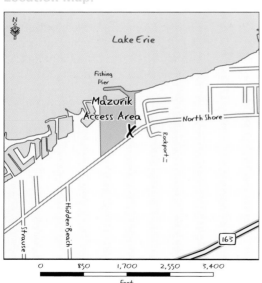

N

Lake Erie

Fishing
Pier

Mazurik
Access Area
X

North Shore

Rockport

Strause

Hidden Beach

163

0   850   1,700   2,550   3,400

Feet

Field Notes:

Date Visited: _____

Learn More:
ODNR Division of Wildlife
ohiodnr.com/wildlife

Marblehead Light

Location:
End of Lighthouse Drive, east of State Route 163 (East Main Street)
110 Lighthouse Drive
Marblehead, OH

Latitude:
N 41° 32.18'

Longitude:
W 082° 42.75'

Waterbody:
Lake Erie

Access Site Type:
Cultural
Educational
Recreational

Environments:
Rocky Shore

Built in 1821, the Marblehead Lighthouse is the oldest continuously operating lighthouse on the Great Lakes. It is also one of the most visited and most photographed landmarks in Lake Erie's Western Basin.

The lighthouse is the centerpiece attraction and namesake for the 13.5-acre state park at the eastern tip of the Marblehead Peninsula. The park offers picnicking and scenic views of Kelleys and South Bass islands and Cedar Point Amusement Park. Other amenities at Marblehead Lighthouse State Park include a handicap-accessible paved path to the lighthouse, restrooms and viewing binoculars.

The exposed limestone bedrock shore is accessible for fishing and scenic viewing. Glacial grooves and striations and numerous types of fossils including Ohio's state fossil, the trilobite, can be found along the shore.

Lighthouse tours are offered between Memorial Day and Labor Day; days and times may vary yearly. A museum, located in the on-site Keeper's House and operated by the Marblehead Lighthouse Historical Society, is open when the tower is open. The U.S. Coast Guard continues to operate and maintain the lighthouse beacon. Today's 300mm lens projects a green signal that flashes every six seconds and is visible for 11 nautical miles.

This state park has received grant funding administered by the Ohio Coastal Management Program for property acquisition and park signage.

ouse State Park

Amenities and Services:

Field Notes:

_____
_____
_____
_____
_____
_____
_____
_____
_____
_____
_____
_____
_____
_____
_____

Location Map:

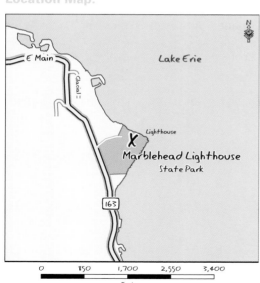

E Main

Glacial

Lake Erie

Lighthouse

X

Marblehead Lighthouse
State Park

163

| 0 | 850 | 1,700 | 2,550 | 3,400 |

Feet

Date Visited: _____

Learn More:

ODNR Division of Parks and Recreation
Marblehead Lighthouse State Park
(419) 734-4424
ohiodnr.com/parks
ohiodnr.com/tabid/763/default.aspx

Lake Point Park

Location:
State Route 163,
near
Lake Breeze Circle
11257 East Bayshore Rd
Marblehead, OH

Latitude:
N 41° 31.63'

Longitude:
W 082° 42.77'

Waterbody:
Lake Erie

**Access
Site Type:**
Recreational

Environments:
Rocky Shore

Located on the southeastern tip of the Marblehead Peninsula, this scenic vista day-use park is just 1.1 miles south of the Marblehead Lighthouse State Park. Lake Point Park's 8.7 acres are on both the west and east sides of Bayshore Road (State Route 163). The Lake Erie shore is accessible on the park's eastern portion for fishing and scenic views of the lake. Park benches overlooking the lake provide views of Cedar Point Amusement Park's skyline.

Lake Point Park's western portion includes all other amenities, including picnic tables, a shelter house, grills, restrooms, a quarry pond, scenic woods, a playground, a covered footbridge and dirt trails. The park is owned and operated by the Danbury Township Trustees.

Amenities and Services:

Location Map:

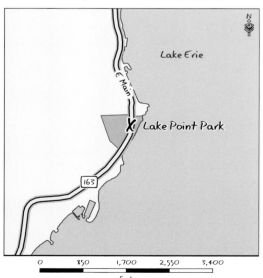

Lake Erie

E Main

X Lake Point Park

163

0   850   1,700   2,550   3,400

Feet

Date Visited: _____

Learn More:
Danbury Township
(419) 732-3039
www.danburytownship.com

Johnson's Island Conf

Location:
S. Confederate Drive,
on Johnson's Island
Marblehead, OH

Latitude:
N 41° 30.04'

Longitude:
W 082° 43.80'

Waterbody:
Sandusky Bay

**Access
Site Type:**
Cultural

Environments:
Rocky Shore

Johnson's Island is a 300-acre island located in Sandusky Bay. The island, which was purchased two-hundred years ago for only $15 and once housed a prisoner-of-war camp, is now subdivided into lots featuring vacation and year-round homes.

Nestled on the east side of the island is the 1.2-acre Johnson's Island Confederate Soldier Cemetery. The cultural site owned by the U.S. Fish and Wildlife Service has no recreational amenities. The solitude and signage provide a glimpse of an era in U.S. history.

In 1861, Johnson's Island was chosen as a Civil War prison used to incarcerate captured Confederate soldiers – primarily officers. The island's fairly isolated, yet easily-accessible location in Sandusky Bay made it an optimal site. The first Confederate prisoners arrived at Johnson's Island in 1862. More than 9,000, and in some estimates up to 15,000, captured soldiers were held at the prison before it was decommissioned in September 1865, at the end of the war.

Today, a black wrought-iron fence surrounds the cemetery of 206 marked grave sites, although the exact number and location of graves is unknown. Three monuments dedicated to the Confederate soldiers who died at Johnson's Island are at the cemetery, the only remaining vestige of the island's prison history.

Johnson's Island is accessible by the manmade Johnson's Island Causeway, which was constructed in 1970. The causeway is south off of East Bayshore Road in Marblehead.

...derate Soldier Cemetery

Amenities and Services:

Location Map:

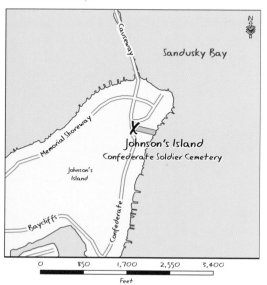

Sandusky Bay

Causeway

Memorial Shoreway

Johnson's Island

Johnson's Island
Confederate Soldier Cemetery

Baycliffs

Confederate

| 0 | 850 | 1,700 | 2,550 | 3,400 |

Feet

Field Notes:

_____

_____

_____

_____

_____

_____

_____

_____

_____

_____

_____

_____

_____

_____

_____

Date Visited: _____

Learn More:
U.S. Fish and Wildlife Service
www.fws.gov/midwest/ohio
or
Johnson's Island Preservation Society
www.johnsonsisland.org

Dempsey State

Location:
Bay Shore Road at Hartshorn Road Danbury Township, OH

Latitude:
N 41° 30.46'

Longitude:
W 082° 45.65'

Waterbody:
Sandusky Bay

Access Site Type:
Outdoor Wildlife

Environments:
Manmade Shore

The 66.8-acre Dempsey State Fishing Access borders Sandusky Bay on the south coast of the Marblehead Peninsula. The site is about 2 miles west of the Johnson's Island Causeway on the south side of South Bayshore Road in Danbury Township.

Similar to the Mazurik Access on the north side of the Marblehead Peninsula, Dempsey Access provides boaters and anglers direct fishing access. Dempsey has a four-lane concrete boat ramp, a semi-protected boat bay, a handicap-accessible L-shaped fishing pier and a small fishing dock. The site provides opportunities for catching fish including smallmouth bass, saugeye, walleye, crappie, catfish and yellow perch.

Dempsey Access has nearly a quarter-mile shore. More than 50 acres at the site are wooded including some areas along the coast. By boat, Dempsey Access is 4.2 miles north of downtown Sandusky (Erie County). The access area has more than 120 car-and-trailer spaces and 45 car-only spaces in a separate lot with handicap accessible paths leading to the fishing pier.

Fishing Access

Amenities and Services:

Location Map:

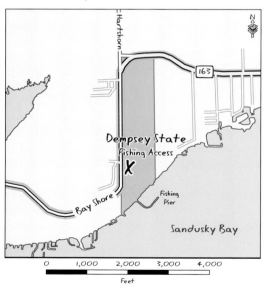

Dempsey State Fishing Access

Sandusky Bay

163

Hartshorn

Bay Shore

Fishing Pier

0   1,000   2,000   3,000   4,000

Feet

Field Notes:

_____

_____

_____

_____

_____

_____

_____

_____

_____

_____

_____

_____

_____

_____

_____

Date Visited: _____

Learn More:
ODNR Division of Wildlife
ohiodnr.com/wildlife

Sandusky Bay B

Location:
End of the old Bay
Bridge Causeway,
near the intersection
of Bay Shore and
Danbury North roads
Danbury Township,
OH

Latitude:
N 41° 29.05'

Longitude:
W 082° 49.76'

Waterbody:
Sandusky Bay

**Access
Site Type:**
Outdoor
Wildlife
Impervious
Pier

Environments:
Manmade Shore

The Sandusky Bay Bridge Access is a state-operated public fishing site approximately 4.2 miles west of Dempsey Fishing Access. The nearly mile long access extending south into the waters of Sandusky Bay was once the northern causeway approach to the former Sandusky Bay Bridge. The former two-lane bridge connected Danbury Township in Ottawa County with the village of Bay View in Erie County. In 1965, the majority of the former bridge's traffic was rerouted west to the new four-lane Thomas A. Edison Memorial Bridge (State Routes 2 and 269).

Prior to the Edison Bridge's completion, the Bay Bridge was the only way for automobile traffic to cross Sandusky Bay. The old bridge featured a lift between the northern and southern causeway approaches, which remained open until 1985. The state removed the bridge's center because of high maintenance costs. Following the center lift's removal, both causeways became popular fishing sites.

Today, on some maps the state fishing access is marked as State Fishing Access/Yetter Road. The fishing access is just east of state Route 269 and south off of East Bayshore Road in Danbury Township.

dge Access

Amenities and Services:

Field Notes:

_____

_____

_____

_____

_____

_____

_____

_____

_____

_____

_____

_____

_____

_____

_____

_____

_____

_____

_____

_____

_____

Location Map:

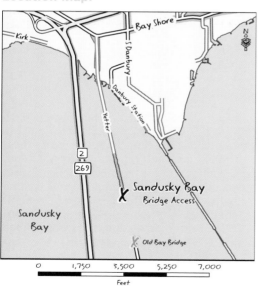

Date Visited: _____

Learn More:
ODNR Division of Wildlife
ohiodnr.com/wildlife

South Bass Isla

Location:
End of Langram Rd
Put-in-Bay
Township, OH

Latitude:
N 41° 37.75'

Longitude:
W 082° 50.45'

Waterbody:
Lake Erie

**Access
Site Type:**
Cultural
Educational

Environments:
Bluff

At the south end of Put-in-Bay Township's Langram Road, the South Bass Island Lighthouse has been guiding vessels through Lake Erie's South Passage since 1897.

Following the 1892 opening of the former Hotel Victory on land currently occupied by South Bass Island State Park, the South Passage became congested. The U.S. Lighthouse Board approved lighthouse construction in 1893.

The South Bass Island Lighthouse is a Queen Anne style brick home with two-and-a-half stories of living space, a full basement and an attached tower. When built, the home was considered very modern with amenities including a laundry room, kitchen range, hot water reservoir, furnace, cistern and hydraulic force pump.

The lighthouse's 60-foot tower was illuminated by a fourth order Fresnel lens until 1962 when the U.S. Coast Guard automated the light. In 1967, The Ohio State University (OSU) assumed care of the home. In 1983, the National Oceanic and Atmospheric Administration installed a meteorological station that enables satellite transmission of weather information to the National Weather Service. In 1990, the lighthouse was added to the National Register of Historic Places. In 1997, permanent ownership of the lighthouse transferred to OSU. The Coast Guard maintains ownership of the tower.

The lighthouse grounds' 3 acres are open for foot traffic. A fence lines the steep bluff along the 894-foot long shore. While exact dates and times vary by year, the lighthouse is open for afternoon tours from late-June to mid-August.

Lighthouse

Amenities and Services:

Field Notes:

_____

_____

_____

_____

_____

_____

_____

_____

_____

_____

_____

_____

_____

_____

_____

Location Map:

South Bass Island
Lighthouse

Lighthouse

Put-in-Bay

Langram

Lake Erie

N

| 0 | 840 | 1,680 | 2,520 | 3,360 |

Feet

Date Visited: _____

Learn More:
Ohio State University
Ohio Sea Grant College Program
(614) 292-8949
ohioseagrant.osu.edu

South Bass Islan

Location:
Catawba Avenue
and Meechen Road
1523 Catawba Ave
Put-in-Bay
Township, OH

Latitude:
N 41° 38.57'

Longitude:
W 082° 50.13'

Waterbody:
Lake Erie

**Access
Site Type:**
Recreational

Environments:
Bluff
Rocky Shore

Pitching a tent and watching the sunset over Lake Erie is encouraged at the 32.8-acre South Bass Island State Park located on the southwest corner of the island so named.

Day-users and those staying overnight have access to park amenities that include picnic tables, grills, shelter house, a playground overlooking Lake Erie and a smooth cobble beach where visitors can wade and swim.

The park has a boat launch ramp and 20 overnight rental docks. A parking lot adjacent to the ramp has 26 car-and-trailer parking spaces. Fishing is allowed from the docks, a small pier and along the beach. Overnight amenities include 125 non-electric campsites, 11 full-service sites, four seasonal cabents, one rustic cabin, modern restrooms and a dump station. Pets are permitted in designated areas. Youth groups of up to 50 people can reserve a group site.

This state park property was the location of the former Hotel Victory, an 180,000 square-foot, 625-room hotel that opened in 1892. When built, it was one of the largest hotels in the world and featured a co-ed swimming pool, a rarity in its time. Fire destroyed the hotel in 1919. Remnants of the swimming pool are still visible in the campground.

The park is at the southern terminus of Catawba Avenue in Put-in-Bay Township. Golf carts, which are street legal on the island, are only permitted to be driven to the park office and are not permitted in the campgrounds.

State Park

Amenities and Services:

Field Notes:

_____

_____

_____

_____

_____

_____

_____

_____

_____

_____

_____

_____

_____

_____

_____

_____

Location Map:

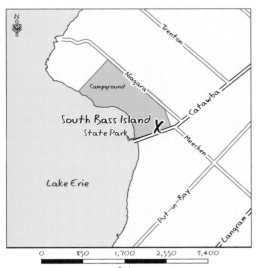

Trenton

Niagara

Campground

Catawba

South Bass Island
State Park

X

Meechen

Lake Erie

Put-in-Bay

Langram

| 0 | 850 | 1,700 | 2,550 | 3,400 |

Feet

Date Visited: _____

Learn More:
ODNR Division of Parks and Recreation
South Bass Island State Park
(419) 285-2112 - seasonally
ohiodnr.com/parks
ohiodnr.com/tabid/753/default.aspx

Captain Parker's

Location:
West Shore
Boulevard at
Trenton Avenue
Put-in-Bay
Township, OH

Latitude:
N 41° 39.05'

Longitude:
W 082° 50.32'

Waterbody:
Lake Erie

**Access
Site Type:**
Scenic

Environments:
Bluff

The 0.45-acre Captain Parker's Park is located at the north-western terminus of Trenton Avenue just past the DuPont Avenue/West Shore Boulevard intersection on the west side of South Bass Island. This scenic overlook site is in Put-in-Bay Township.

Captain Alfred Parker, once the skipper of a popular island ferry, served as a Put-in-Bay Township trustee for more than 30 years.

Behind a low wooden barrier preventing farther car/golf cart access, a mowed-grass green space is heavily shaded by deciduous trees. Each tree is surrounded by a planter box which doubles as seating. Along with a picnic table placed near the top of the limestone bluff, the planter boxes allow for views of Green Island and Lake Erie sunsets. For safety, the top of the bluff is lined with a chain-link fence prohibiting water access and signed "No swimming."

Park

Amenities and Services:

Location Map:

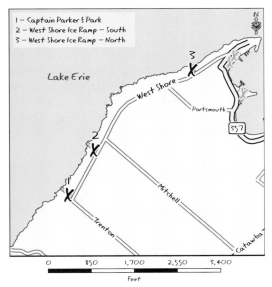

1 – Captain Parker's Park
2 – West Shore Ice Ramp – South
3 – West Shore Ice Ramp – North

Lake Erie

West Shore

Portsmouth

357

Mitchell

Trenton

Catawba

0   850   1,700   2,550   3,400
Feet

Field Notes:

_____

_____

_____

_____

_____

_____

_____

_____

_____

_____

_____

_____

_____

_____

_____

_____

Date Visited: _____

Learn More:
Put-in-Bay Township
(419) 285-2292
www.pibtownship.com

West Shore Ice Ra

Location (north):
West Shore Boulevard, northeast of Portsmouth Road Put-in-Bay Township, OH

Location (south):
West Shore Boulevard, southwest of Mitchell Road Put-in-Bay Township, OH

Lat/long (north):
N 41° 39.47'
W 082° 49.78'

Lat/long (south):
N 41° 39.20'
W 082° 50.20'

Access Site Type:
Impervious

Manmade Shore
Rocky Shore

South Bass Island's two public ice ramps are both located on the west side of South Bass Island along West Shore Boulevard in Put-in-Bay Township.

Grants in 1998 and 1999 from the Ohio Coastal Management Program funded, in part, renovations and improvements to the southern ice ramp to provide access for ice fisherman, eliminate safety hazards, and rebuild the ice ramp and emergency boat launch.

The 0.06-acre West Shore Ice Ramp North is about 625 feet east of the Portsmouth Avenue intersection. The site is a 20-foot wide strip of land extending 160 feet at a northwest bearing from the road to Lake Erie. The access has no amenities and is predominantly used as a fishing site and kayak livery.

The 0.34-acre West Shore Ice Ramp South is 335 feet south and west of the Mitchell Road intersection. The impervious surface site is 55 feet wide and 275 feet from the road edge to the water. The site is marked on the north by a line of deciduous trees and on the south by a wooden split-rail fence.

mps

Amenities and Services (north):

 P

Amenities and Services (south):

 P

Location Map:

1 – Captain Parker & Park
2 – West Shore Ice Ramp – South
3 – West Shore Ice Ramp – North

Lake Erie

West Shore

Portsmouth

357

Mitchell

Trenton

Catawba

N

| 0 | 850 | 1,700 | 2,550 | 3,400 |

Feet

Ottawa County

Field Notes:

_____
_____
_____
_____
_____
_____
_____
_____
_____
_____
_____
_____
_____
_____
_____
_____
_____

Date Visited: _____

Learn More:
Put-in-Bay Township
(419) 285-2292
www.pibtownship.com

Put-in-Bay Aquat

Location:
SR 357 and
West Shore Blvd
Put-in-Bay, OH

Lat/Long (Visitor):
N 41° 39.52'
W 082° 49.60'

Lat/Long (Peach):
N 41° 39.50'
W 082° 49.61'

Waterbody:
Lake Erie

**Access
Site Type (Visitor):**
Cultural
Educational

**Access
Site Type (Peach):**
Educational

Environments:
Manmade Shore

The 1-acre Put-in-Bay Aquatic Visitors Center allows face-to-face interaction with live Lake Erie creatures. Housed in a former state fish hatchery, the center's goal is to provide people an opportunity to bond with Lake Erie. The center has six aquariums filled with Lake Erie fish, microscopes to view plankton and other organisms and hands-on exhibits highlighting Ohio fish species, fisheries management, invasive species, fish anatomy and the old hatchery's operations.

The state hatchery closed in 1988. In 1992 the ODNR Division of Wildlife transformed it into the Aquatic Visitors Center. The Ohio State University's Ohio Sea Grant Program took over management in 2009, while maintaining a partnership with the Division of Wildlife. Admission is free. The center's public fishing dock loans out fishing equipment and bait. Benches, a small picnic area and courtesy dockage are also available. This site is open seasonally in summer.

Adjacent to the west is Stone Laboratory's nearly 1-acre Peach Point Research Facility, a former federal fish hatchery. It is home to the Lab's summer research program. In 2010, research areas include exotic and threatened species, harmful algal blooms, hypoxic dead zone phenomena and other water quality issues. The building is only open to the public during annual open house events. There is an educational kiosk and an Ohio Historical Marker located on the grounds.

Visitors Center
and Peach Point Research Facility

Amenities and Services (Visitors Center):

Amenities and Services (Peach Point):

Field Notes:

_____

_____

_____

_____

_____

_____

_____

_____

_____

_____

_____

_____

_____

_____

_____

Location Map:

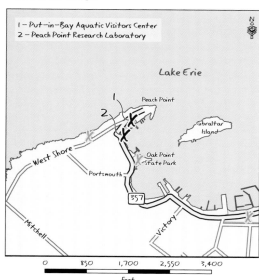

1 – Put–in–Bay Aquatic Visitors Center
2 – Peach Point Research Laboratory

Lake Erie

Peach Point

Gibraltar Island

West Shore

Oak Point State Park

Portsmouth

357

Mitchell

Victory

N

0   850   1,700   2,550   3,400
Feet

Date Visited: _____

Learn More:
Ohio State University
Ohio Sea Grant College Program,
Aquatic Visitors Center
(440) 808-5627
ohioseagrant.osu.edu/avc

Oak Point State

Location:
Bayview Drive at
Portsmouth Avenue
Put-in-Bay, OH

Latitude:
N 41° 39.39'

Longitude:
W 082° 49.56'

Waterbody:
Lake Erie

**Access
Site Type:**
Recreational

Environments:
Manmade Shore

The smallest Ohio State Park occupies just 1.5 acres on Ohio's most visited Lake Erie island – South Bass.

Despite its small size, Oak Point State Park's location provides panoramic views of the bustling Put-in-Bay harbor and surrounding attractions including Perry's Victory and International Peace Memorial, Stone Lab on Gibraltar Island and the Aquatic Visitors Center.

The park, located on Bayview Drive (State Route 357) in Put-in-Bay Township, is a half-mile walk west from downtown Put-in-Bay. This day-use park offers a picnic area, fishing access, overnight docking facilities, a small parking lot, restrooms and a vending machine.

The park occupies a triangular piece of land that points into the harbor toward Gibraltar Island. The north face of the triangle is lined with a bulkhead and topped with a narrow sidewalk suitable to fish from. The south face is lined with boat slips.

Oak Point State Park is one of the five state parks on Ohio's Lake Erie islands. The other island state parks include Kelleys, Middle Bass, North Bass and South Bass. Green Island, located west of South Bass Island, is a state wildlife refuge that is accessible by permit only.

Park

Ottawa County

Amenities and Services:

Location Map:

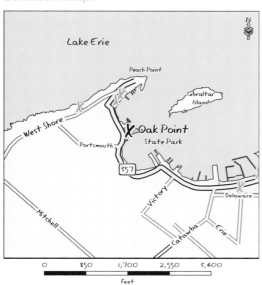

Lake Erie

Peach Point

Gibraltar Island

Oak Point
State Park

West Shore

Portsmouth

357

Victory

Delaware

Mitchell

Catawba

Erie

N

| 0 | 850 | 1,700 | 2,550 | 3,400 |

Feet

Field Notes:

Date Visited: _____

Learn More:
ODNR Division of Parks and Recreation
South Bass Island & Oak Point state
parks
(419) 285-2112 - seasonally
ohiodnr.com/parks
ohiodnr.com/tabid/753/default.aspx

DeRivera Park
Put-in-Bay Village Marina and Beach

Location (Park):
Bounded by
Delaware Avenue,
Hartford Avenue,
Catawba Avenue and
Bayview Drive
Put-in-Bay, OH

Lat/Long (Park):
N 41° 39.20'
W 082° 49.06'

Waterbody (All):
Lake Erie

**Access
Site Type (Park):**
Recreational

**Environments
(Park):**
Manmade Shore

The 7-acre DeRivera Park is in the heart of downtown Put-in-Bay. Shaded by old-growth trees, the park features a limestone fountain, war memorials, playground equipment, picnic tables, benches and a public bathhouse.

North of Bayview Drive (State Route 357) is the park's public "B" dock, operated by the DeRivera Trust. On either side are public docks "A" and "C," which are operated by the village of Put-in-Bay. Flanking the public docks are many private businesses offering dock rental. In 2009, daily and overnight rates for the public docks were $1.60 per running foot; personal watercraft and rafts were $5 each. Electricity and water are available. Rafting, up to four vessels, is mandatory.

The L-shaped "C" dock, on the harbor's east side is 765 feet. The middle "B" dock's main pier is 430 feet; a secondary pier is 140 feet. On the west, "A" dock's main pier is 475 feet; a secondary pier is 155 feet. The public may walk the length of each dock. A wide, handicap accessible sidewalk with numerous benches runs the length of the harbor.

Neither swimming nor floating toys are allowed in the marina. However, the village's 95-foot sand beach is a quarter mile away at the east terminus of Delaware Avenue. The beach is marked on the south by a cement-block groin and on the north by the seawall protecting national park lands. The only sign denoting the public beach states: "No Lifeguard on Duty." The beach has no amenities.

Amenities and Services (Park):

Amenities and Services (Marina):

Amenities and Services (Beach):

Location Map:

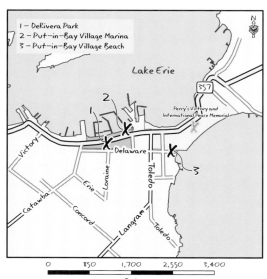

1 – DeRivera Park
2 – Put-in-Bay Village Marina
3 – Put-in-Bay Village Beach

Lake Erie

357

Perry's Victory and
International Peace Memorial

Victory

Delaware

Erie

Loraine

Toledo

Catawba

Concord

Langram

Toledo

0   850   1,700   2,550   3,400
Feet

Location (Marina):
Bayview Drive, (SR 357) just
west of Hartford Avenue
intersection

Lat/Long (Marina):
N 41° 39.25'
W 082° 48.98'

**Access
Site Type (Marina):**
Recreational
Impervious/Pier

Environments (Marina):
Manmade Shore

Location (Beach):
Eastern end of Delaware
Avenue

Lat/Long (Beach):
N 41° 39.17'
W 082° 48.77'

**Access
Site Type (Beach):**
Recreational
Right-of-Way

Environments (Beach):
Sandy Beach

Learn More:
Put-in-Bay Chamber of Commerce
www.visitputinbay.com

Ottawa County

Perry's Victory and Int

Location:
93 Delaware Avenue
Put-in-Bay, OH

Latitude:
N 41° 39.25'

Longitude:
W 082° 48.67'

Waterbody:
Lake Erie

Access Site Type:
Cultural
Educational

Environments:
Manmade Shore

Constructed between 1912 and 1915 by a commission of nine states and the federal government, Perry's Victory & International Peace Memorial was built to commemorate the United States naval triumph in the Battle of Lake Erie during the War of 1812 and to celebrate the long-lasting peace between Great Britain, Canada and the United States. The 352-foot tall Doric column is the third tallest U.S. memorial and is just 5 miles south of the US-Canada border, the longest undefended international border in the world.

Six officers slain during the battle are buried under the memorial's rotunda. Its observation platform is 317 feet above Lake Erie. An elevator takes visitors to the platform from where, on a clear day, one can see Cleveland's skyline 60 miles to the east.

The 23.9 acres of park grounds span the width of the South Bass Island at its narrowest point. Both the north and south sides have poured concrete seawalls with flat tops which one can walk or sit on and enjoy the view.

In 1936, the memorial became part of the National Park Service. The park's Visitor Center, opened in 2002, hosts interpretative displays, reenactment movies and a book store. Beginning in 2010, the memorial column will be closed for approximately 2 years for restoration. The visitor center and park grounds will remain open and park staff will offer new interpretive tours.

national Peace Memorial

Amenities and Services:

Location Map:

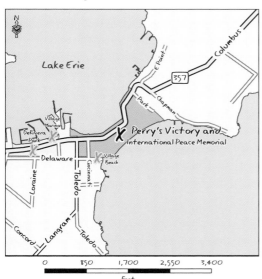

Lake Erie

Village Marina

DeRivera Park

Delaware

Loraine

Toledo

Cincinnati

Village Beach

Concord · Langram

Toledo

Park

E Prant

357

Columbus

Chapman

X Perry's Victory and International Peace Memorial

```
0        850     1,700    2,550    3,400
                  Feet
```

Field Notes:

_____

_____

_____

_____

_____

_____

_____

_____

_____

_____

_____

_____

_____

_____

_____

_____

Date Visited: _____

Learn More:
Perry's Victory and International
Peace Memorial
(419) 285-2184
www.nps.gov/pevi

Scheeff East Poin

Location:
End of SR 357
eastern terminus
Put-in-Bay, OH

Latitude:
N 41° 39.89'

Longitude:
W 082° 47.71'

Waterbody:
Lake Erie

Access Site Type:
Natural

Environments:
Rocky Shore
Sandy Beach

In 2008, the 9-acre Scheeff East Point Nature Preserve became the first property owned by the Put-in-Bay Township Park District. The land was purchased with federal Endanged Species Act funding and donations from numerous partners including the Western Reserve Land Conservancy, and many community members including the Scheeff-family for which the park is named.

Beside rows of grapevines, the preserve's land entrance is at the northeastern tip of South Bass, near the end of State Route 357. The entrance is marked by three boulders and a combination split-rail and chain-link fence that makes the property only accessible to foot-traffic from dawn to dusk.

Foot paths, cut through meadow plants and tall grasses, lead around the perimeter of the peninsula-shaped preserve to the shore. The preserve provides habitat for thousands of migratory birds, numerous species of butterflies and the Lake Erie watersnake.

What appears as a white sand beach is a product of Lake Erie's waves grinding 20 years of invasive zebra and quagga mussel shells into tiny fragments. Stones of various shapes and sizes are mixed in with the crushed shells and native sand; footwear is recommended. The water level around East Point is extremely shallow, only deep enough for kayakers and canoes to paddle ashore. The preserve offers views of various other islands.

Nature Preserve

Amenities and Services:

Field Notes:

_____

_____

_____

_____

_____

Location Map:

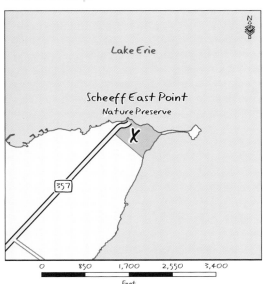

Lake Erie

Scheeff East Point
Nature Preserve

357

0   850   1,700   2,550   3,400
Feet

Date Visited: _____

Learn More:
Put-in-Bay Township Park District
(419) 285-4772
or
Black Swamp Conservancy
Lake Erie Islands Chapter
www.lakeerieislandsbsc.com/nature

Middle Bass Isla

Ottawa County

Location:
Fox Road, S.
Middle Bass Island
1719 Fox Road
Put-in-Bay
Township, OH

Latitude:
N 41° 40.42'

Longitude:
W 082° 48.69'

Waterbody:
Lake Erie

**Access
Site Type:**
Recreational

Environments:
Bluff
Rocky Shore
Manmade Shore
Sandy Beach

The 136-acre Middle Bass Island State Park is comprised of a series of parcels along the south, southeast and west sides and a few inland areas of the island so named.

Middle Bass is accessible by boat, public ferry and airplane. The majority of parkland is accessible from Fox Road, which runs from the public ferry dock north through the center of the 770.5-acre island.

The park features a mile of coastal access and an expanded marina which opened in mid-summer 2009. The marina can dock up to 190 boats, providing island residents seasonal dockage and transient dock space for visitors. Design and construction of a bathhouse is underway. The marina's entrance is on the east side of the island. Primitive camping is available.

Along the park's south side is the former Lonz Winery building. This site was used for wine production, storage and dance halls from 1863 until July 1, 2000, when the winery closed.

The park also includes natural areas with endangered plant and wildlife species, wetlands, pocket beaches and unique glacial grooves and striations. As of March 2010, ODNR is reviewing the park's site plan and seeking public/private partnerships for development.

90   *Lake Erie Public Access Guidebook*

d State Park

Amenities and Services:

Location Map:

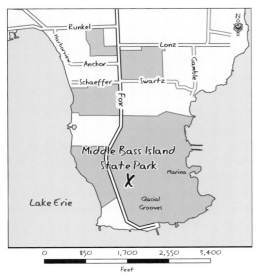

Middle Bass Island State Park

Lake Erie

Glacial Grooves

Marina

Runkel
Harborview
Lonz
Anchor
Gamble
Schaeffer
Swartz
Fox

0   850   1,700   2,550   3,400
Feet

Field Notes:

_____
_____
_____
_____
_____
_____
_____
_____
_____
_____
_____
_____
_____
_____
_____
_____

Date Visited: _____

Learn More:
ODNR Division of Parks and Recreation
Middle Bass Island State Park
(419) 285-0311 - seasonally
ohiodnr.com/parks
ohiodnr.com/tabid/766/default.aspx

Petersen Woods and K

Location:
Fox and Deist roads,
northern Middle
Bass Island
Put-in-Bay
Township, OH

Lat/Long (Petersen):
N 41° 41.41′
W 082° 48.23′

Lat/Long (Kuehnle):
N 41° 41.32′
W 082° 48.23′

Waterbody:
Lake Erie

**Access
Site Type:**
Natural
Outdoor
Wildlife

**Environments
(Petersen):**
Sandy Beach

**Environments
(Kuehnle):**
Manmade Shore

The nearly 2-acre Petersen Woods and 20-acre Kuehnle State Wildlife Area are adjacent to each other on Deist Road where Middle Bass narrows, just north of the island's airport.

Petersen Woods has 300 feet of road frontage but narrows as it approaches the water and has just a 98 foot shore. The woods provide habitat for mammals, song and wading birds and the Lake Erie watersnake. Future site plans include nature trails, a boardwalk and observation platform; however, as of March 2010 the site had no amenities. A sign on Deist Road identifies the site which was acquired in 2004 by the Black Swamp Conservancy's Lake Erie Islands Chapter.

Kuehnle State Wildlife Area is called "The Marsh" by islanders. The site features a large wetland and marsh-swamp suitable for bird watching and photography. The habitat provides a resting area for songbirds, raptors, waterfowl and wading birds that migrate across western Lake Erie. It also harbors a number of threatened and endangered plants, rare salamanders, Blandings turtles and the Lake Erie watersnake. The triangular-shaped wildlife area has two sides fronting Lake Erie. The 0.28-mile north side overlooks North Bass Island. The 0.25-mile southeast side affords views of South Bass and Kelleys islands. Both shores are structurally reinforced with dikes and accessible for fishing.

hnle State Wildlife Area

Amenities and Services (Woods):

Amenities and Services (Kuehnle):

Location Map:

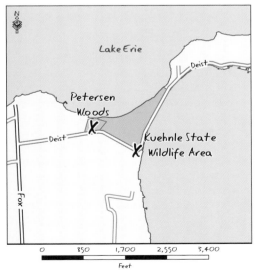

Field Notes:

_____

_____

_____

_____

_____

_____

_____

_____

_____

_____

_____

_____

_____

_____

_____

_____

_____

Date Visited: _____

Learn More:
Black Swamp Conservancy
Lake Erie Islands Chapter
www.lakeerieislandsbsc.com/nature
or
ODNR Division of Wildlife
ohiodnr.com/wildlife

North Bass Isla[nd]

Location:
Kenny and
Meires roads
Put-in-Bay
Township, OH

Latitude:
N 41° 42.48'

Longitude:
W 082° 48.93'

Waterbody:
Lake Erie

**Access
Site Type:**
Outdoor
Wildlife

Environments:
Rocky Shore
Wetland

The 593 public acres on North Bass Island help preserve Lake Erie's largest undeveloped island as a wildlife area and state park. The ODNR owns and manages 87 percent of the 677-acre island.

As part of a comprehensive vision for resource protection and recreation across the entire Lake Erie Islands region, North Bass Island State Park is only open to primitive camping with a special permit, hiking, picnicking, biking, wildlife watching and similar low-impact outdoor pursuits. Fishing is allowed in appropriate places along the island's 4.1 miles of public shore.

In the future, trails are planned to connect key points of interest including the island's historic chapel and cemetery, and landmarks such as the Simon Fox and Gottesman houses. ODNR continues to lease 38 acres to Sandusky's Firelands Vineyard to preserve North Bass Island's cultural fabric and history of vineyards and winemaking.

North Bass Island, also known as Isle St. George, is the northern-most island in Ottawa County. It is located 18 miles from the Ohio mainland and less than 2 miles from the Canadian border. There is no ferry service to North Bass Island. The island is only accessible via airplane and personal watercraft.

The public areas on North Bass Island were purchased with state funds and grants from the Department of the Interior Land and Water Conservation Fund and the Coastal and Estuarine Land Conservation Program, which is now administered by the ODNR Office of Coastal Management.

State Park

Amenities and Services:

Field Notes:

_____

_____

_____

_____

_____

_____

_____

_____

_____

_____

_____

_____

_____

_____

_____

Location Map:

Lake Erie

Wires

Peeple

Tuhan

Tuhan

Kenny

Meires

North Bass Island
State Park
X

N

| 0 | 1,250 | 2,500 | 3,750 | 5,000 |

Feet

Date Visited: _____

Learn More:
ODNR Division of Parks and Recreation
Lake Erie Islands State Park
(419) 797-4530
ohiodnr.com/parks

Established: February 12, 1820
2000 Population: 61,792
2010 Projection: 59,940
Land Area and Rank: 409.2 square miles, 66 of 88
County Seat: City of Fremont
Named for: Native American word meaning "cold water"

Miles of Coast: 13 miles
Miles of Publicly Accessible Coast: 3.5 miles
Number of Access Sites: 1

Sandusky County

A brief history:

Sandusky County was established on February 12, 1820, and named after a Native American term for "at the cold water." Sandusky County was originally part of territory set aside for Ohio's Native American people by the Treaty of Greenville. White settlement of the county occurred very slowly, due to the Great Black Swamp occupying most of the land.

A small portion of the county's northern border lies along Lake Erie's Sandusky Bay. The largest city and county seat is Fremont. Ninety-seven percent of the county's 409 square miles are rural, and 75 percent of the land is cultivated. Agriculture and farming is Sandusky County's largest employment sector; the county is the fifth largest producer of tomatoes in Ohio. Manufacturing businesses, service industries and retail positions finish second, third and fourth respectively among ways county residents earn a living.

The 19th President of the United States, Rutherford B. Hayes ranks as one of Sandusky County's most prominent former residents. His home, Spiegel Grove, is now a historical landmark operated by the Ohio Historical Society.

Learn More:

Sandusky County
www.sandusky-county.org

**Chamber of Commerce
Sandusky County**
www.scchamber.org

**Sandusky County Convention
and Visitors Bureau**
www.lakeeriesfavoriteneighbor.com

Sandusky County Park District
www.scpd-parks.org

Public Access Management:

State	1

Incorporated Areas   Unincorporated Areas   1 in = 11 miles

Pickerel Creek St[

Location:
U.S. Route 6 at
County Road 256
3451 County Road 256
Riley Township, OH

Latitude:
N 41° 25.06'

Longitude:
W 082° 57.25'

Waterbody:
Sandusky Bay

Access Site Type:
Outdoor
Wildlife

Environments:
Manmade Shore
Rocky Shore
Sandy Beach
Wetland

The 3,200 acre Pickerel Creek State Wildlife Area includes 3.47 miles of Sandusky Bay's south shore in Townsend and Riley townships. This is Sandusky County's only public access site on Lake Erie.

The ODNR Division of Wildlife acquired Pickerel Creek in 1987. The majority of the site has been restored to wetlands with the remainder in woods, brush and native grasses. Pickerel Creek flows through the western half of the area, forming a high quality freshwater estuarine habitat. Additional Lake Erie tributaries flow through the wildlife area including Raccoon, South and Green creeks.

The wildlife area's parcels are all north of U.S. Route 6. The largest contiguous property begins on the west side of County Road 280 (Duffet Road) extending to County Road 250 (Minier Road). This area provides access to Sandusky Bay. A system of dikes is maintained here and accessible for walking/hiking. The wildlife area is intended for fishing, hunting, trapping and wildlife viewing.

The wildlife area's two smaller sections are not coastal and located to the west off of County Road 265 (Ohms Road). The area's headquarters and check-in station are off County Road 256 (Pearson Road). An observation tower located north of U.S. Route 6 near County Road 260 is open year-round for viewing the abundant wetland wildlife.

e Wildlife Area

Amenities and Services:

Location Map:

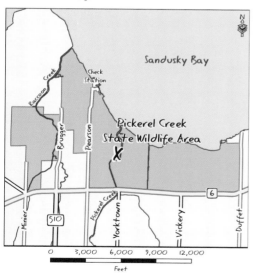

Sandusky Bay

Check Station

Raccoon Creek

Brugger

Pearson

Pickerel Creek State Wildlife Area
X

Pickerel Creek

Miner

510

Yorktown

Vickery

Duffet

6

0   3,000   6,000   9,000   12,000

Feet

Field Notes:

_____

_____

_____

_____

_____

_____

_____

_____

_____

_____

_____

_____

_____

_____

_____

_____

Date Visited: _____

Learn More:
ODNR Division of Wildlife
Pickerel Creek State Wildlife Area
(419) 547-6007
ohiodnr.com/tabid/19789/default.aspx

Established: March 16, 1838
2000 Population: 79,551
2010 Projection: 81,420
Land Area and Rank: 254.5 square miles, 87 of 88
County Seat: City of Sandusky
Named for: Erie Native American Tribe

Miles of Coast: 68 miles
Miles of Publicly Accessible Coast: 9.6 miles
Number of Access Sites: 39

Erie County

A brief history:

Erie County's first inhabitants included the Erie, Iroquois, Wyandot and Ottawa Indians.

In 1792, the Connecticut Legislature established the "Fire Lands" (later condensed to one word, "Firelands") in the westernmost portion of the Connecticut Western Reserve. The Firelands consisted of present-day Erie and Huron counties, as well as Danbury and a part of Catawba Island townships in Ottawa County and Ruggles Township in Ashland County. The Firelands had been reserved for Connecticut residents whose homes had been burned down during British raids in the late 1700s (Revolutionary War). In the early 1800s, settlers began populating the area. In 1809, Huron County was established and comprised the entire Firelands.

With population growth, the Ohio Legislature split Huron County in 1838, creating Erie County out of the northern land. Erie County quickly became a transportation hub through the creation of the Mad River & Lake Erie Railroad in 1835 and the Milan Canal in 1839. The area was also a center for ship building, fishing, ice cutting and lumber imports.

Sandusky, the county seat, was platted in 1818 in the shape of the Masonic symbol. Blackboard chalk was invented in the city in 1835. Corrugated cardboard was also invented in Sandusky; and the city is believed to have the largest collection of limestone buildings in Ohio.

More than 50 percent of the county's land is used for farming. Tourism attracts millions of visitors annually to locals attractions including Cedar Point Amusement Park, the area's unique museums, outdoor recreation sites and ferry transport to the Lake Erie islands.

Learn More:

Erie County
www.erie-county-ohio.net

City of Huron
www.cityofhuron.org

City of Sandusky
www.ci.sandusky.oh.us

City of Vermilion
www.vermilion.net

Erie County Chamber of Commerce
www.eriecountyohiocofc.com

Huron Chamber of Commerce
www.huron.net

Huron Township
www.hurontwp.org

Kelleys Island
Chamber of Commerce
www.kelleysislandchamber.com

Lake Erie Shores & Islands (East)
www.shoresandislands.com

Margaretta Township
www.margarettatwp.org

Sandusky Main Street Association
www.sanduskymainstreet.com

Vermilion Chamber of Commerce
vermilionohio.com

Vermilion Township
www.vermiliontownship.com

Village of Kelleys Island
www.kelleysisland.us

Public Access Management:

Local	25
State	8
Metropark	5
Other	1

Incorporated Areas   Unincorporated Areas   1 in = 11 miles

Willow Point State

Location:
Wahl Road, east of
Whites Landing
Margaretta Township

Latitude:
N 41° 26.09'

Longitude:
W 082° 52.32'

Waterbody:
Sandusky Bay

**Access
Site Type:**
Outdoor
Wildlife

Environments:
Rocky Shore
Sandy Beach
Manmade Shore

Providing access to a half-mile of Sandusky Bay's shore, the 645-acre Willow Point State Wildlife Area is located on the north and south sides of Wahl Road seven miles west of Sandusky. Land for the wildlife area straddles Erie and Sandusky counties, but the portion abutting the bay is entirely in Erie County.

Prior to 1850, the area was an extensive wet prairie where grasses densely grew seven feet high and were bound together with pea vines. Traveling through was nearly impossible. The vast prairies were surrounded by oak-chestnut woodlots. Wild rice and other waterfowl foods grew in abundance in Sandusky Bay's clear water. After the land was settled, cleared and drained for agriculture, the waterfowl habitat was damaged.

From approximately 1920 to 1972 a group of sportsmen leased the marsh and called it the Willow Point Duck Club. When high water levels in the early 1970s caused severe problems with maintaining the marsh, the club disbanded. The ODNR Division of Wildlife acquired Willow Point in 1975.

Today, there are no recreational amenities at Willow Point which is managed as a public hunting and fishing area, with emphasis on waterfowl and rabbits. About two-thirds of the wildlife area is open water and marshland; cattails are the primary vegetation. Shore fishing is permitted and an unmarked, gravel access road leads visitors to Sandusky Bay.

Wildlife Area

Field Notes:

_____

_____

_____

_____

_____

_____

_____

_____

_____

_____

_____

_____

_____

Location Map:

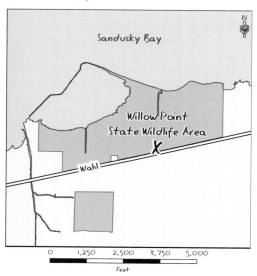

Sandusky Bay

Willow Point
State Wildlife Area
X

Wahl

| 0 | 1,250 | 2,500 | 3,750 | 5,000 |

Feet

Erie County

Date Visited: _____

Learn More:
ODNR Division of Wildlife
ohiodnr.com/wildlife
ohiodnr.com/tabid/20103/default.aspx

Sandusky Bay B

Location:
Bayview and
Bayside drives
Bay View, OH

Latitude:
N 41° 28.72'

Longitude:
W 082° 49.66'

Waterbody:
Sandusky Bay

**Access
Site Type:**
Outdoor
Wildlife
Impervious
Pier

Environments:
Manmade Shore

Erie County

The former southern causeway approach to the Sandusky Bay Bridge is a popular publicly accessible fishing site in the Erie County village of Bay View. Shown as "Yetter Road" on some maps including those maintained by the Erie County Auditor's Office, the southern causeway is 2,080 feet long.

The former Bay Bridge once spanned Sandusky Bay connecting Bay View with Danbury Township in Ottawa County. In 1965, the majority of the former bridge's traffic was rerouted west to the new four-lane Thomas A. Edison Memorial Bridge (State Routes 2 and 269). Prior to the new, wider and higher bridge's completion, the old bridge was the only way for automobile traffic to cross Sandusky Bay.

Dedicated in 1929, the bridge featured a lift between the northern and southern causeway approaches. At the time of its construction, it was the longest bridge and causeway in Ohio. The bridge was privately financed by the Sandusky Bay Bridge Company; the state of Ohio took ownership of the bridge in 1936. The bridge remained open until 1985 when the state removed the steel center because of the high cost of maintenance. Following the center lift's removal, both the north causeway in Ottawa County and this south causeway became popular fishing sites.

The southern causeway can be accessed from Bayview Drive in Bay View. A street sign at the causeway's Bayview Drive intersection identifies the former bridge approach as Bayside Drive.

dge – South

Amenities and Services:

Location Map:

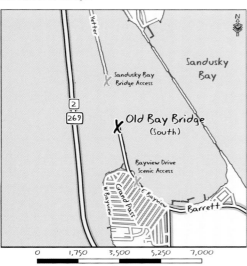

Erie County

Field Notes:

_____
_____
_____
_____
_____
_____
_____
_____
_____
_____
_____
_____
_____
_____
_____
_____

Date Visited: _____

Bayview Drive S

Location:
Alongside
Bayview Drive
Bay View, OH

Latitude:
N 41° 28.33'

Longitude:
W 082° 49.48'

Waterbody:
Sandusky Bay

**Access
Site Type:**
Scenic

Environments:
Manmade Shore

The Bayview Drive Scenic Access is a linear strip of green space stretching for 2,175 feet, which is just under a half mile, along the northeast side of East Bayview Drive in the village of Bay View.

This site is primarily an overlook. It is unmarked, unnamed and owned by Bay View Village.

Bay View Village Hall is at the south end of Old Bay Bridge fishing access site. The scenic overlook stretches from Village Hall in a southeast direction to where East Bayview Drive becomes Barrett Road and intersects with Martins Point Road.

The site features minimal amenities. They include a picnic table and numerous park benches facing the waters of Sandusky Bay.

enic Access

Amenities and Services:

Location Map:

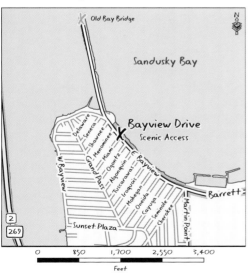

Old Bay Bridge

Sandusky Bay

Bayview Drive
Scenic Access

Delaware
Seneca
Shawnee
Menominee
Miami
W Bayview
Grand Pass
Ogontz
Algonquin
Tuscarawas
Bayview
Mohegan
Oneida
Cayuga
Seminole
Cherokee
Martin Point
Barrett

2
269

Sunset Plaza

| 0 | 850 | 1,700 | 2,550 | 3,400 |

Feet

Field Notes:

Date Visited: _____

Erie County

Lions Park

Location:
La Salle Street, north of Monroe Street
Sandusky, OH

Latitude:
N 41° 26.89′

Longitude:
W 082° 44.80′

Waterbody:
Sandusky Bay

Access Site Type:
Recreational

Environments:
Manmade Shore

The 13-acre Lions Park is located on the city of Sandusky's west side north of the intersection of West Monroe and La Salle streets. Winnebago Avenue provides access to the park; however signs mark the park's entrance and parking at La Salle Street.

Lions Park provides traditional recreation activities, including picnic shelters and tables, playground equipment, restrooms and basketball courts. A steep bluff of concrete rubble leads the able-footed down to the 912-foot shore on Sandusky Bay. At times, depending on water levels and wind direction, the shore may have a narrow strip or pockets of mixed sand, cobble and invasive zebra and quagga mussel shells. Shore fishing is allowed; however, a sign near the water warns that access to the shore should be done at one's own risk.

As of March 2010, the city is developing a new master plan for the park. The proposed plan includes transforming the waterfront to include an accessible public beach, long walking paths, a summer splash pad which will turn into a winter ice rink, an event lawn and potentially a boardwalk extending into the bay.

Lions Park debuted as Winnebago Park in July 1912 and became Lions Park in July 1928. It is the second park ever associated with the Lions Club International.

Amenities and Services:

Location Map:

Field Notes:

_____
_____
_____
_____
_____
_____
_____
_____
_____
_____
_____
_____
_____
_____
_____
_____
_____
_____

Erie County

Date Visited: _____

Learn More:
City of Sandusky
Parks and Recreation
(419) 627-5844
www.ci.sandusky.oh.us

Sandusky Bay Pa

Location:
End of Mills Street
Sandusky, OH
and
End of Wayne Street
Sandusky, OH

Lat/Long (Mills):
N 41° 27.06'
W 082° 43.67'

Lat/Long (Wayne):
N 41° 27.50'
W 082° 42.65'

Waterbody:
Sandusky Bay

**Access
Site Type:**
Recreational
Scenic

Environments:
Manmade Shore

Erie County

The Sandusky Bay Pathway is a linear park providing direct access and waterfront views to the city of Sandusky's coast throughout the downtown area.

Extending from the northern terminus of Mills Street on the city's west side, the pathway connects various public parks, piers and vistas before ending on the city's east side at the southeast corner of Washington and Meigs streets beside the City Hall building.

Construction of the pathway began in 2003 on the east side of the city. The pathway has increased in length westward to its current distance of just over 2 miles.

Starting in the west, the pathway connects coastal access sites including the Shelby Street Boat Launch, Chesapeake Walkway, Jackson Street Pier, Schade-Mylander Plaza, Shoreline Park, Sandusky Bay Pavilion, Meigs Street Pier, Battery Park, Springer's Wharf and the Washington Street Pier. A scenic overlook site is also at Wayne Street.

The Sandusky Bay Pathway Master Plan, funded in part by grants from the Ohio Coastal Management Program, specifies a route to extend the pathway to more than 13 miles of waterfront recreational paths.

No motorized vehicles, except wheelchairs, are allowed on the handicap accessible pathway. Cyclists and skaters must yield the right-of way to pedestrians. Pets must be on leashes. Most of the pathway is lighted by street lamps for 24-hour use. Benches and other amenities are found at various stops.

...thway

Location Map (Mills Street):

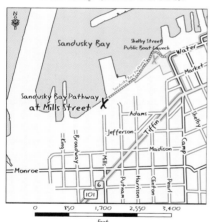

Location Map (Wayne Street):

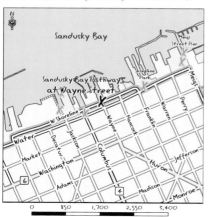

Amenities and Services:

Field Notes:

_____

_____

_____

_____

_____

_____

_____

_____

_____

_____

_____

_____

_____

_____

Date Visited: _____

Learn More:
City of Sandusky
Parks and Recreation
(419) 627-5844
www.ci.sandusky.oh.us

Erie County

Shelby Street Pu

Location:
Shelby and
Water streets
101 Shelby Street
Sandusky, OH

Latitude:
N 41° 27.25'

Longitude:
W 082° 43.40'

Waterbody:
Sandusky Bay

**Access
Site Type:**
Recreational

Environments:
Manmade Shore

The Shelby Street Public Boat Launch is located at the corner of Water and Shelby streets just west of downtown Sandusky. This site provides a free public boat launch and offers at least seven structures that extend into the bay providing fishing access. A waterside paved trail and a handicap accessible observation deck provide scenic views of Sandusky Bay. This site includes picnic tables and a seasonally operated concession store.

The boat launch has four lanes. The main boat launch parking lot is approximately 6.2 acres with more than 100 car-and-trailer parking spots. An additional 2.3-acre parking lot just to the south on Shelby Street offers an additional 58 car and car-and-trailer spaces.

In 2001, an Ohio Coastal Management Program grant funded, in part, the construction of a handicap accessible fishing pier/observation deck here. In 2009, the Shelby Street Boat Launch was the launch site for nine fishing tournaments from May to November including some that were nationally televised.

The Sandusky Bay Pathway, a multi-purpose trail accessible to bicyclists, walkers, roller bladers, etc., meanders through the boat launch as it connects Mills Street to the west and Shoreline Drive points to the east.

SHELBY STREET
PUBLIC BOAT LAUNCH

lic Boat Launch

Amenities and Services:

Location Map:

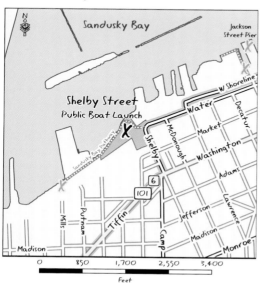

Sandusky Bay

Jackson Street Pier

Shelby Street
Public Boat Launch

W Shoreline

Water
Decatur
Market
McDonough
Washington
Shelby
Adams
Sandusky Bay Parkway
6
101
Lawrence
Jefferson
Putnam
Tiffin
Madison
Mills
Camp
Madison
Monroe

| 0 | 850 | 1,700 | 2,550 | 3,400 |

Feet

Field Notes:

_____

_____

_____

_____

_____

_____

_____

_____

_____

_____

_____

_____

_____

_____

_____

Erie County

Date Visited: _____

Learn More:
City of Sandusky
Parks and Recreation
(419) 627-5844
www.ci.sandusky.oh.us

Chesapeake Walk

Location:
West Shoreline Drive
at Jackson Street
Sandusky, OH

Latitude:
N 41° 27.46'

Longitude:
W 082° 42.89'

Waterbody:
Sandusky Bay

**Access
Site Type:**
Scenic

Environments:
Manmade Shore

Erie County

The Chesapeake Walkway is a handicap-accessible path that surrounds the Chesapeake Building in the city of Sandusky's emerging Paper District.

The 950-foot walkway, completed in 2009, occupies the northern exterior of the land along the 400 block of West Shoreline Drive from Decatur Street on the west to Jackson Street on the east. The Chesapeake Lofts private luxury condominiums occupy the building that overlooks Sandusky Bay and the shipping channel.

The building was constructed by Hinde & Dauch Paper Co. in the early 1920s. Hinde and Dauch Paper Co. invented corrugated cardboard boxes and at one time was the largest producer of them worldwide. The building was more recently occupied by Chesapeake Display, a company specializing in producing point-of-purchase displays. Chesapeake Display closed in 1992. The building, listed by the National Register of Historic Places for its significance in industrial history, sat vacant for more than a decade.

In 2003, Sandusky used a $3 million grant from the Clean Ohio Fund for Brownfield Revitalization for acquisition, demolition and remediation of the Paper District's waterfront properties.

The Paper District remains under development as the city considers various plans, including those to turn some of the vacant land adjacent to the Chesapeake Walkway into parks that would pay tribute to the city's historical connection to the paper packaging industry.

...way

Amenities and Services:

Location Map:

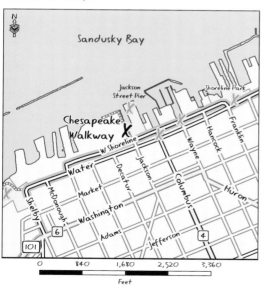

Sandusky Bay

Jackson Street Pier

Shoreline Park

Chesapeake Walkway

W Shoreline

Water

Decatur

Jackson

Wayne

Hancock

Franklin

Columbus

Huron

Market

McDonough

Shelby

Washington

Adams

Jefferson

6

101

4

0   840   1,680   2,520   3,360

Feet

Erie County

Field Notes:

_____

_____

_____

_____

_____

_____

_____

_____

_____

_____

_____

_____

_____

_____

_____

_____

_____

_____

Date Visited: _____

Learn More:
City of Sandusky
Parks and Recreation
(419) 627-5844
www.ci.sandusky.oh.us

Jackson Street

Location:
West Shoreline Drive,
at the end of
Jackson Street
Sandusky, OH

Latitude:
N 41° 27.53′

Longitude:
W 082° 42.88′

Waterbody:
Sandusky Bay

**Access
Site Type:**
Scenic
Recreational
Impervious
Pier

Environments:
Manmade Shore

Erie County

Located on West Shoreline Drive at Jackson Street, the nearly 4-acre Jackson Street Pier is locally popular for fishing while catching scenic views across Sandusky Bay of Johnson's Island, the Marblehead Peninsula and Cedar Point Amusement Park.

This site is a large impervious surface parking lot with a paved walkway around much of the pier's perimeter. The pier's rectangular shape affords 825 feet of waterline access. The pier is also the docking/boarding site for the Goodtime I, Jet Express and Pelee Islander ferry boats which seasonally transport passengers to the islands.

Jackson Street Pier is located in downtown Sandusky and is adjacent to the west of the G.A. Boeckling Building, which once served as Cedar Point's winter headquarters. The building now houses the ODNR Office of Coastal Management.

The shipping channel is just north of the pier. During the shipping season, Great Lakes freighters pass just yards north of the pier. The pier and surrounding waters are also used for training by the city's safety services.

The Sandusky Bay Pathway runs along the pier's south end. An Erie County Historic Marker noting historical significance of Johnson's Island as a Civil War Prison camp (*see Ottawa County*) is located here. During summer months, the city charges a fee for overnight parking at the pier.

Pier

Amenities and Services:

Location Map:

N

Sandusky Bay

Jackson
Street Pier

Shoreline Park

W Shoreline

Franklin

Hancock

Wayne

Jackson

Water

Decatur

Columbus

Huron

McDonough

Market

Shelby

Washington

6

Adams

4

| 0 | 850 | 1,700 | 2,550 | 3,400 |

Feet

Erie
County

Field Notes:

Date Visited: _____

Learn More:
City of Sandusky
Parks and Recreation
(419) 627-5844
www.ci.sandusky.oh.us

Schade—Mylander

Location:
West Shoreline Drive
at Columbus Avenue
Sandusky, OH

Latitude:
N 41° 27.44'

Longitude:
W 082° 42.74'

Waterbody:
Sandusky Bay

**Access
Site Type:**
Scenic

Environments:
Manmade Shore

Erie
County

The Schade-Mylander Plaza is located at the northern terminus of Columbus Avenue north of Water Street in downtown Sandusky. The majority of the plaza is between Shoreline Drive and Water Street; however the coastal access portion is on the north side of Shoreline Drive. This 140-foot section affords Sandusky Bay fishing access.

The Sandusky Bay Pathway passes through plaza grounds parallel to Shoreline Drive. This portion of Shoreline Drive is closed to vehicle traffic during the seasonal, Friday night summer concert series and for various other events held in the plaza.

A large fountain occupies the center of the Schade-Mylander Plaza which is landscaped in a tiered manner to afford park-bench style seating on the cement pads which also serve as flower planters. There are no regular amenities at the plaza; however, seasonally and during special events, vendors are present.

Plaza

Amenities and Services:

Location Map:

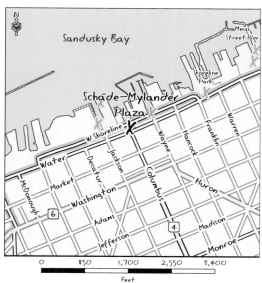

Sandusky Bay

Schade-Mylander Plaza

Meigs Street Pier

Shoreline Park

W Shoreline

Water

Market

McDonough

Decatur

Jackson

Washington

Adams

Jefferson

Columbus

Wayne

Hancock

Franklin

Warren

Huron

Madison

Monroe

6

4

0   850   1,700   2,550   3,400

Feet

Erie

Field Notes:

_____
_____
_____
_____
_____
_____
_____
_____
_____
_____
_____
_____
_____
_____
_____
_____
_____
_____
_____
_____

Date Visited: _____

Learn More:
City of Sandusky
Parks and Recreation
(419) 627-5844
www.ci.sandusky.oh.us

Shoreline Park

Location:
East Shoreline Drive
and Water Street
411 East Water Street
Sandusky, OH

Latitude:
N 41° 27.56'

Longitude:
W 082° 42.43'

Waterbody:
Sandusky Bay

**Access
Site Type:**
Recreational

Environments:
Manmade Shore

The 8-acre Shoreline Park occupies land of three former industrial-commercial piers north of the intersection of East Shoreline Drive and Water Street in downtown Sandusky.

As early as 1846, piers were known to exist at Shoreline Park. The piers were used to ship iron ore, grain, lumber, sand, crushed stone and packaged freight. Ferry boats and barges wintered at the piers, last used in 1973.

Today, this site offers many amenities including a picnic shelter where the railroad roundhouse once was, tables, restroom facilities, playground equipment, drinking fountains, walking paths, a concession stand, sculptures and ample parking affording scenic views of Sandusky Bay.

In 2001, an Ohio Coastal Management Program grant funded, in part, the construction of a handicap-accessible fishing station/observation deck at the northwest corner of the park's western pier. Fishing is also allowed from the entire shore area, which occupies nearly 3,700 feet of accessible waterline due to the site's layout on the former piers.

Shoreline Park is on the Sandusky Bay Pathway; bike rentals are seasonally available at the park's concession stand. The park is adjacent to the east of the ODNR Division of Wildlife's Sandusky Fish Research Station and Law Enforcement Office.

Field Notes:

_____

_____

_____

Amenities and Services:

Location Map:

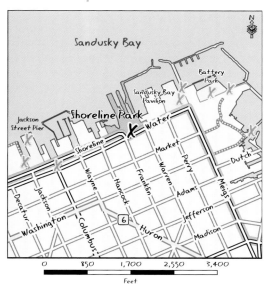

Sandusky Bay

Battery Park

Sandusky Bay Pavilion

Shoreline Park

Water

Jackson Street Pier

Shoreline

Market

Wayne

Franklin

Hancock

Warren

Perry

Adams

Meigs

Dutch

Decatur

Jackson

Washington

Columbus

6

Huron

Jefferson

Madison

| 0 | 850 | 1,700 | 2,550 | 3,400 |

Feet

Date Visited: _____

Learn More:
City of Sandusky
Parks and Recreation
(419) 627-5844
www.ci.sandusky.oh.us

Sandusky Bay Pa

Location:
Meigs and
Water streets
Sandusky, OH

Latitude:
N 41° 27.67′

Longitude:
W 082° 42.22′

Waterbody:
Sandusky Bay

**Access
Site Type:**
Recreational

Environments:
Manmade Shore

Erie County

The Sandusky Bay Pavilion is an outdoor entertainment complex used by the city of Sandusky primarily to host special events. The 5.3 acres at the northwest corner of Meigs and Water streets is the former home of the Surf's Up Wave Action Pool. Although still on park grounds, the pool area was closed in 2004 because it was no longer financially sustainable.

The Sandusky Bay Pathway runs the length of the pavilion's southern boundary. Pavilion grounds afford views of Cedar Point Amusement Park, Sandusky Bay, Johnson's Island and the Marblehead Peninsula.

Sandusky Bay Pavilion's grounds are predominately mowed grass. Amenities at the pavilion include a picnic shelter and tables, playground equipment and restrooms. Fishing access is available along the rectangular shaped land parcel's 8,500-foot waterline.

...vilion

Amenities and Services:

Location Map:

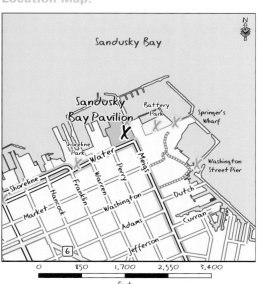

Field Notes:

_____

_____

_____

_____

_____

_____

_____

_____

_____

_____

_____

_____

_____

_____

_____

_____

_____

_____

_____

Date Visited: _____

Learn More:
City of Sandusky
Parks and Recreation
(419) 627-5844
www.ci.sandusky.oh.us

Meigs Street Pier

Location:
End of Meigs Street
Sandusky, OH

Latitude:
N 41° 27.71'

Longitude:
W 082° 42.21'

Waterbody:
Sandusky Bay

**Access
Site Type:**
Recreational
Impervious
Pier

Environments:
Manmade Shore

The Meigs Street Pier provides a one-third-mile fishing access along the publicly accessible pedestrian pier. The handicap accessible pier is predominately poured concrete extending north and then veering east from the north terminus of Meigs Street. The pier marks the western and eastern side of a private marina. Portions of the marina are separated from the pier with chain-link fence.

Mounted binoculars at Meigs Street Pier offer closer views of the Marblehead Peninsula, Cedar Point Amusement Park and Sandusky Bay. Water along the western side of the Meigs Street Pier is deep enough to provide dockage to various transient tourist attractions, such as the smaller Tall Ships when they visit Sandusky.

Field Notes:

_____

_____

_____

_____

Amenities and Services:

Location Map:

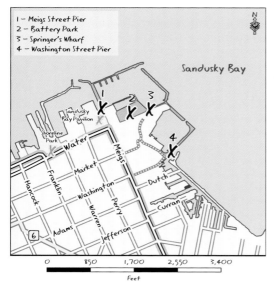

1 – Meigs Street Pier
2 – Battery Park
3 – Springer's Wharf
4 – Washington Street Pier

Sandusky Bay

Sandusky Bay Pavilion

Shoreline Park

Water

Meigs

Market

Franklin

Washington

Hancock

Perry

Warren

Dutch

Curran

Adams

Jefferson

6

0   850   1,700   2,550   3,400
Feet

_____

_____

_____

_____

_____

_____

_____

_____

Date Visited: _____

Learn More:
City of Sandusky
Parks and Recreation
(419) 627-5844
www.ci.sandusky.oh.us

Battery Park

Location:
Meigs and
Water streets
Sandusky, OH

Latitude:
N 41° 27.69'

Longitude:
W 082° 42.09'

Waterbody:
Sandusky Bay

**Access
Site Type:**
Recreational

Environments:
Manmade Shore

The 3.1 acres of land at Battery Park are located at the northeast corner of Meigs and Water streets. The park is predominantly an open green space shaded by old-growth deciduous trees and surrounded by marinas and parking lots. The park includes a quarter-mile paved blacktop loop path that is part of the Sandusky Bay Pathway.

Park amenities include a picnic shelter and tables, grills, playground equipment and benches overlooking the marinas and Sandusky Bay.

Direct access to Sandusky Bay is obstructed by a chain-link fence; however fishing access is available within walking distance at the adjacent piers and wharf. Battery Park's history includes being the 1835 groundbreaking site for Ohio's second railroad, the Mad River and Lake Erie Railroad.

Erie
County

Field Notes:

Amenities and Services:

Location Map:

1 — Meigs Street Pier
2 — Battery Park
3 — Springer's Wharf
4 — Washington Street Pier

Sandusky Bay

Sandusky Bay Pavilion

Shoreline Park

Water

Meigs

Market

Franklin

Hancock

Washington

Warren

Percy

Adams

Jefferson

Dutch

Curran

6

| 0 | 850 | 1,700 | 2,550 | 3,400 |

Feet

Date Visited: _____

Learn More:
City of Sandusky
Parks and Recreation
(419) 627-5844
www.ci.sandusky.oh.us

Springer's Wharf

Location:
Meigs and Water
streets, East of
Battery Park
Sandusky, OH

Latitude:
N 41° 27.70'

Longitude:
W 082° 42.01'

Waterbody:
Sandusky Bay

**Access
Site Type:**
Impervious
Pier

Environments:
Manmade Shore

Erie County

The foot of Springer's Wharf extends from the eastern terminus of East Water Street east of Battery Park into Sandusky Bay. The handicap accessible paved concrete fishing access provides a walkway between a private marina to the north and a private sailing club to the south.

The wharf is a T-shaped structure with the walkway and northern extent measuring a quarter-mile. The southern wharf area runs along the northeast end of the Sadler Sailing Basin and measures nearly one-tenth of a mile. The wharf has no amenities.

The wharf affords views of Cedar Point Amusement Park and the eastern portion of Sandusky Bay. This offshore area is popular with ice boat sailors. Ice boats glide on top of the frozen bay water on what looks like three large ice skates. During summer months, the waters are used by learn-to-sail programs and by various boats of all sizes.

Field Notes:

_____

_____

_____

_____

_____

_____

_____

_____

_____

_____

_____

_____

_____

_____

_____

_____

_____

_____

Amenities and Services:

Location Map:

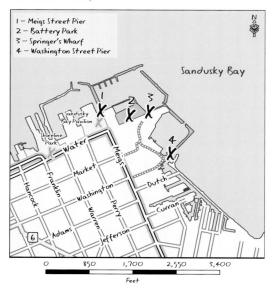

1 – Meigs Street Pier
2 – Battery Park
3 – Springer's Wharf
4 – Washington Street Pier

Sandusky Bay

O   850   1,700   2,550   3,400
Feet

Erie County

Date Visited: _____

Learn More:
City of Sandusky
Parks and Recreation
(419) 627-5844
www.ci.sandusky.oh.us

Washington Stre

Location:
End of Washington Street, east of Meigs Street Sandusky, OH

Latitude:
N 41° 27.56′

Longitude:
W 082° 41.91′

Waterbody:
Sandusky Bay

Access Site Type:
Impervious Pier

Environments:
Manmade Shore

The foot of the Washington Street Pier begins behind the City Hall and Sandusky Police Station complex. The handicap accessible poured concrete pier extends into the eastern part of Sandusky Bay providing nearly a quarter mile of fishing access around the southern portion of the Saddler Sailing Basin. The Washington Street Pier is partially shaded by deciduous trees. The site has few amenities.

The pier affords excellent views of Cedar Point Amusement Park and the eastern portion of Sandusky Bay. This offshore area is popular with ice boat sailors. Ice boats glide on top of the frozen bay water on what looks like three large ice skates. During summer months, the waters are used by learn-to-sail programs and by various boats of all sizes.

+ Pier

Amenities and Services:

Location Map:

1 – Meigs Street Pier
2 – Battery Park
3 – Springer's Wharf
4 – Washington Street Pier

N

Sandusky Bay

Sandusky Bay Pavilion

Shoreline Park

Water
Meigs
Market
Franklin
Hancock
Washington
Perry
Warren
Adams
Jefferson
Dutch
Curran

6

| 0 | 850 | 1,700 | 2,550 | 3,400 |

Feet

Field Notes:

Date Visited: _____

Learn More:
City of Sandusky
Parks and Recreation
(419) 627-5844
www.ci.sandusky.oh.us

Pipe Creek State

Erie County

Location:
F Street and
River Avenue
Sandusky, OH

Latitude:
N 41° 26.94'

Longitude:
W 082° 40.03'

Waterbody:
East Sandusky Bay

**Access
Site Type:**
Outdoor
Wildlife

Environments:
Manmade Shore
Wetland

The Pipe Creek State Wildlife Area is a manmade marsh originally known as the Big Island Wetlands. Located behind the city of Sandusky's Big Island water treatment facility, it was built to mitigate the loss of adjacent wetlands by private developers. Control and management of Pipe Creek was assumed by the ODNR Division of Wildlife in 1991.

The majority of the 97-acre site is a diked marsh divided into four, shallow-water management areas and surrounded on three sides by East Sandusky Bay. The marsh areas, varying from one to three feet deep, are managed for wetland wildlife.

Pipe Creek includes a small wooded area leading to the flat-topped dikes. The dikes are good wildlife viewing areas as they are 8-10 feet above water level. Fishing in the bay is allowed along the outer dikes.

The only hunting allowed at Pipe Creek is waterfowl, by special permit from an annual drawing. Trapping is not permitted during the waterfowl season but is allowed during the remainder of the legal furbearer season.

There is a colony of common tern at Pipe Creek. The common tern is an Ohio endangered species that is protected from disturbance during spring and summer nesting. Signage prohibiting entry in nesting areas will be posted.

Pipe Creek is located on F Street which is accessible from both First and River streets. The parking lot, at the corner of River and F streets, also serves the Big Island Preserve

Wildlife Area

Amenities and Services:

Erie County

Field Notes:

_____

_____

_____

_____

_____

_____

_____

_____

_____

_____

_____

_____

_____

_____

_____

Location Map:

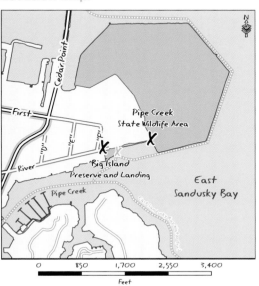

Date Visited: _____

Learn More:
ODNR Division of Wildlife
ohiodnr.com/wildlife
ohiodnr.com/tabid/20028/default.aspx

Big Island Preser

Erie County

Location:
F Street and
River Avenue
Sandusky, OH

Latitude:
N 41° 26.92′

Longitude:
W 082° 40.24′

Waterbody:
East Sandusky Bay

**Access
Site Type:**
Recreational

Environments:
Riparian/River
Rocky Shore
Manmade Shore
Wetland

The Big Island Preserve and Landing is located adjacent to the Pipe Creek State Wildlife Area on F Street in the city of Sandusky.

The landing is a canoe and kayak launch site designed to provide access to the 15-mile East Sandusky Bay Water Trail. The landing is mapped as the first livery point on the water trail, which was dedicated in June 2007. A printable map and water trail guide can be found at: ohiodnr.com/tabid/2899/default.aspx, which is an ODNR Division of Watercraft Webpage.

The East Sandusky Bay Water Trail is also recognized as a "blueway." Blueways are routes along a river or across other bodies of water such as a lake or bay designed for people using small, beachable, hand-powered watercraft like kayaks, canoes or rowboats.

On land, dirt paths at the Big Island Preserve lead to fishing areas along this manmade structure.

This site is not easily identifiable as "Big Island Preserve and Landing." Signage is present near the dirt path leading to the launch site. However, the parking lot at the corner of River and F streets, which serves both the landing and the Pipe Creek State Wildlife Area, only has signage recognizing the wildlife area. F Street is accessible from both River and First streets.

...e and Landing

Amenities and Services:

Field Notes:

_____

_____

_____

_____

Location Map:

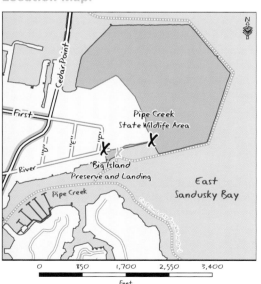

Cedar Point

First

"D" "E"

River

Pipe Creek
State Wildlife Area

X X X

"Big Island"
Preserve and Landing

Pipe Creek

East
Sandusky Bay

N

0   850   1,700   2,550   3,400

Feet

Erie County

_____

_____

_____

_____

_____

_____

_____

_____

_____

_____

Date Visited: _____

Learn More:
Erie MetroParks
(419) 625-7783
www.eriemetroparks.com

East Sandusky B

Location:
U.S. Route 6, west of
Perkins Avenue
3819 Cleveland Road
Huron Township, OH

Latitude:
N 41° 25.56'

Longitude:
W 082° 38.56'

Waterbody:
East Sandusky Bay

**Access
Site Type:**
Natural

Environments:
Wetland

Erie
County

The 92-acre East Sandusky Bay MetroPark (ESB) is one of four neighboring parks owned by Erie MetroParks along U.S. Route 6 (Cleveland Road) between the cities of Huron and Sandusky. ESB is in the northwest portion of these park's 1,200 coastal acres collectively managed as the East Sandusky Bay Preserve MetroParks.

The mouth of Plum Brook and its backwaters form the greater part of this preserve bordering East Sandusky Bay. A recent biological survey found more than 180 plant species at this site, including 50 native species that depend on wet or moist habitats for survival. ESB is a critical habitat for breeding and migrating birds and ducks, providing a stop to rest and refuel before crossing Lake Erie. The site has had 14 successful eagle nests during the last 18 years.

The mile-long natural surface trail leads from a paved parking area through woods and fields to the marsh. The half-mile East Bay Trail leads to an observation overlook and a trailhead for the East Sandusky Bay Water Trail. The preserve also features the Stockdale Arboretum and a picnic area. There are no onsite restrooms or drinking water.

ESB was formerly known as the Community Foundation Preserve at Eagle Point and includes the East Sandusky Bay MetroPark Extension, an area that was once the site of the Sandusky Drive-in Theatre. The theatre site is being reclaimed to a natural state. These lands were acquired in part with a grant from the Coastal and Estuarine Land Conservation Program, which is administered by the ODNR Office of Coastal Management.

Lake Erie Public Access Guidebo

y MetroPark

Amenities and Services:

Location Map:

East Sandusky Bay

Future Water Trail Access

East Sandusky Bay Metropark

X

6

E Bayview

Bayfield

Arboretum

Joseph Steinen Wildlife Area

X

Perkins

| 0 | 1,000 | 2,000 | 3,000 | 4,000 |

Feet

Field Notes:

_____

_____

_____

_____

_____

_____

_____

_____

_____

_____

_____

_____

_____

_____

_____

_____

Date Visited: _____

Learn More:
Erie MetroParks
(419) 625-7783
www.eriemetroparks.com

Erie County

Joseph Steinen W

Location:
U.S. Route 6, west of
Perkins Avenue
Huron Township, OH

Latitude:
N 41° 25.33′

Longitude:
W 082° 38.21′

Waterbody:
East Sandusky Bay

**Access
Site Type:**
Outdoor
Wildlife
Natural

Environments:
Rocky Shore
Manmade Shore
Wetland

Erie
County

The 141-acre Steinen Wildlife Area is one of four neighboring parks owned by the Erie MetroParks. The wildlife area is in the middle portion of 1,200 coastal acres collectively known as the East Sandusky Bay Preserve MetroParks.

Steinen is comprised of three separate parcels, all adjacent to U.S. Route 6 (Cleveland Road) between the cities of Huron and Sandusky. The east and west parcels are bounded on the north by East Sandusky Bay; a private motel property is located in between. Steinen's southern parcel does not provide coastal access, but features Erie County's Ohio Bicentennial Barn. It is bounded by U.S. Route 6 to the north and Perkins Avenue to the south.

The northern portions of the east and west parcels are influenced by East Sandusky Bay's water level and at times are underwater. Steinen's marsh area, similar to other area marshes, is in the process of being reclaimed from the invasive phragmites.

Steinen's east and west parcels feature meadow and wooded areas with a network of meandering trails. The trails may be closed seasonally during bald eagle nesting. A picnic table is near the gravel parking area. Fishing, seasonal hunting and trapping are allowed.

Steinen was acquired in part with a grant from the Coastal and Estuarine Land Conservation Program, which is administered by the ODNR Office of Coastal Management.

dlife Area

Amenities and Services:

Location Map:

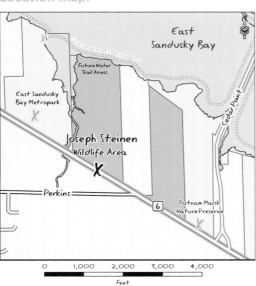

East Sandusky Bay

Future Water Trail Access

East Sandusky Bay Metropark

Joseph Steinen Wildlife Area

Perkins

Cedar Point

Putnam Marsh Nature Preserve

6

0   1,000   2,000   3,000   4,000

Feet

Field Notes:

Date Visited: _____

Learn More:
Erie MetroParks
(419) 625-7783
www.eriemetroparks.com

Putnam Marsh Na

Location:
U.S. Route 6 at the
Cedar Point Chaussee
Huron Township, OH

Latitude:
N 41° 25.09'

Longitude:
W 082° 37.65'

Waterbody:
East Sandusky Bay

**Access
Site Type:**
Natural

Environments:
Wetland

The 966-acre Putnam Marsh Nature Preserve is one of four neighboring parks owned by the Erie MetroParks. Putnam's 90 land acres are in two disjoined parcels both north of U.S. Route 6 and are connected by the preserve's ownership interest in East Sandusky Bay. Putnam Marsh is part of Erie MetroPark's 1,200 collective coastal acres known as the East Sandusky Bay Preserve MetroParks.

Putnam's northwest parcel is on the east side of Hemminger Ditch and adjacent to the Sandusky Griffing Airport property. In the spring, a controlled burn may be used to help eradicate the invasive Phragmites that grow in this portion of the marsh. Putnam's southeast land parcel is adjacent to the east of the Steinen Wildlife Area's east parcel.

The marsh, renowned for its abundant waterfowl, is an important stopping site for migratory birds. Parts of the marsh are seasonally hunted, by special permit, in a program co-managed by Erie MetroParks and the ODNR Division of Wildlife. Fishing in East Sandusky Bay is permitted.

Putnam Marsh is open daily, year-round from 8 a.m. to dusk, unless otherwise posted. A parking lot off Cleveland Road near Cedar Point Road is planned; however, as of March 2010 no parking, no potable water and no restroom facilities are available in the preserve. These lands were acquired in part with a grant from the Coastal and Estuarine Land Conservation Program, which is administered by the ODNR Office of Coastal Management.

...ture Preserve

Amenities and Services:

Location Map:

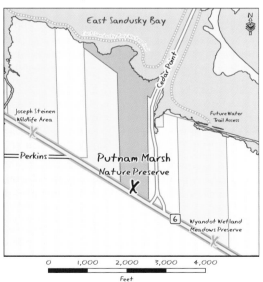

East Sandusky Bay

Cedar Point

Joseph Steinen
Wildlife Area

Perkins

Future Water
Trail Access

Putnam Marsh
Nature Preserve
X

6 Wyandot Wetland
Meadows Preserve

```
0    1,000   2,000   3,000   4,000
              Feet
```

Field Notes:

_____

_____

_____

_____

_____

_____

_____

_____

_____

_____

_____

_____

_____

_____

_____

_____

_____

Erie
County

Date Visited: _____

Learn More:
Erie MetroParks
(419) 625-7783
www.eriemetroparks.com

Wyandot Wetland

Location:
U.S. Route 6, east of
Cedar Point Chaussee
Huron Township, OH

Latitude:
N 41° 24.86'

Longitude:
W 082° 37.21'

Waterbody:
East Sandusky Bay

**Access
Site Type:**
Natural

Environments:
Wetland

Erie
County

The 84-acre Wyandot Wetland Meadows Preserve is one of a group of neighboring parks owned by the Erie MetroParks. Wyandot is the easternmost of the 1,200 collective coastal acres known as the East Sandusky Bay Preserve MetroParks.

Wyandot, acquired by the MetroParks in 2006, is located north of U.S. Route 6 (Cleveland Road) between the cities of Huron and Sandusky. The preserve is just east of Cedar Point Road and adjacent to the west of a private nursery. The preserve provides coastal access to the portion of East Sandusky Bay that is part of Sheldon Marsh State Nature Preserve.

The majority of Wyandot's acres are being reclaimed from row-crop farmland to native prairie meadow vegetation. The northern portion of the property includes a narrow strip of woods adjacent to marshland. The marshland area is influenced by the water level of East Sandusky Bay and at times may be underwater.

Wyandot is intended as a natural wildlife viewing site. These lands were acquired in part with a grant from the Coastal and Estuarine Land Conservation Program, which is administered by the ODNR Office of Coastal Management. There are presently no amenities at the preserve.

Meadows Preserve

Amenities and Services:

Location Map:

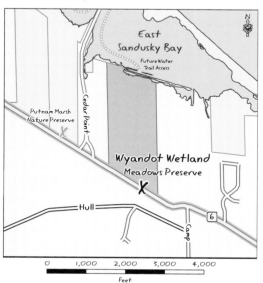

East Sandusky Bay

Future Water Trail Access

Cedar Point

Putnam Marsh Nature Preserve

Wyandot Wetland Meadows Preserve

Hull

Camp

6

| 0 | 1,000 | 2,000 | 3,000 | 4,000 |

Feet

Field Notes:

_____
_____
_____
_____
_____
_____
_____
_____
_____
_____
_____
_____
_____
_____
_____

Date Visited: _____

Learn More:
Erie MetroParks
(419) 625-7783
www.eriemetroparks.com

Sheldon Marsh Sta

Location:
U.S. Route 6, west of
Rye Beach Road
2715 Cleveland Rd, West
Huron Township, OH

Latitude:
N 41° 24.50'

Longitude:
W 082° 36.13'

Waterbody:
Lake Erie
East Sandusky Bay

**Access
Site Type:**
Natural

Environments:
Barrier Beach
Sandy Beach
Wetland

Erie
County

The 463-acre Sheldon Marsh State Nature Preserve is one of the last remaining undeveloped stretches of coast on Lake Erie's south shore. Acquired by ODNR in 1979, Sheldon Marsh is Ohio's best example of a natural barrier beach.

The 1.13-mile barrier beach used to extend from the NASA Plum Brook water intake pump station (still present) westward. Then in 1972, the west-end of the barrier beach was separated from the rest of the 6.5-mile Cedar Point sand spit due to a rise in lake level coupled with a major northeast storm. Over the past 40 years, the barrier beach has eroded westward and lakeward approximately 1,200 feet in places, forming a broad U-shaped bay and shrinking the marshland behind.

Still, the preserve's lush wetlands provide protection and habitat for a variety of plants and animals including 300 bird species. During migrations, Neotropicals, shorebirds and waterfowl briefly stop to rest and feed in the cattail marsh, swamp forest, upland hardwood forest and old-field habitats of the preserve. The preserve's wetlands mark the eastern end of East Sandusky Bay and are one of Ohio's three remaining coastal wetlands not diked for water level management.

The preserve's parking lot is north of U.S. Route 6 about 4 miles west of downtown Huron. A handicap-accessible asphalt paved path connects the parking lot to a boardwalk leading to the barrier beach. Various wetland overlooks are along the path. The preserve is open 365-days a year from

e Nature Preserve

Amenities and Services:

Field Notes:

_____
_____
_____
_____
_____
_____
_____
_____
_____
_____
_____
_____
_____
_____
_____
_____
_____
_____

Location Map:

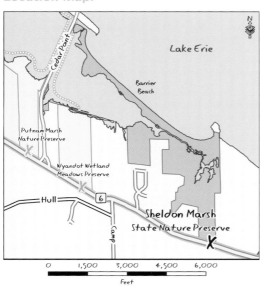

Lake Erie

Cedar Point

Barrier Beach

Putnam Marsh Nature Preserve

Wyandot Wetland Meadows Preserve

Hull 6

Camp

Sheldon Marsh State Nature Preserve

| 0 | 1,500 | 3,000 | 4,500 | 6,000 |

Feet

Date Visited: _____

Learn More:
ODNR Division of
Natural Areas and Preserves
ohiodnr.com/dnap
ohiodnr.com/tabid/910/default.aspx

Waterplant Beach

Location:
West Drive at
Sail Away Drive,
north of South St
Huron , OH

Latitude:
N 41° 23.96'

Longitude:
W 082° 33.43'

Waterbody:
Lake Erie

**Access
Site Type:**
Recreational

Environments:
Sandy Beach

Erie
County

The half-acre Waterplant Beach is west of West Drive's northern terminus, which is accessible from South Street in Huron. The public area is north of the city's 12-acre Service Complex. It is less than one-fifth a mile west of Lake Front Park.

Visitors to Waterplant Beach must cross the shallow, narrow mouth of the Washburn Ditch which has a 3-plus-acre estuary area south of the beach. An estuary is a partially enclosed waterbody near a river or stream mouth where flowing tributary water meets and mixes with the water of a lake or ocean. In this case, depending on water levels, the mouth of the Washburn Ditch estuary may be closed by a sand bar separating the natural tributary from the open lake waters.

Water levels also affect the length of this foot-friendly sand beach. It can range from 350 feet to nearly 700 feet long and is widest at its eastern end. The back of the publicly accessible area is marked by deciduous trees and vegetation growing atop a concrete rubble revetment.

The site has a picnic table and a beach safety water rescue box. Swimming is at one's own risk. Very limited street parking is available. The beach closes at dusk.

Field Notes:

_____

_____

_____

_____

_____

Amenities and Services:

_____

_____

_____

_____

_____

_____

Location Map:

_____

_____

_____

_____

_____

_____

_____

_____

_____

Date Visited: _____

Learn More:
City of Huron
(419) 433-5000
www.cityofhuron.org

Lake Front Park

Location:
Block of Center,
Ohio and Park streets
Huron, OH

Latitude:
N 41° 23.90'

Longitude:
W 082° 33.26'

Waterbody:
Lake Erie

**Access
Site Type:**
Recreational

Environments:
Sandy Beach
Manmade Shore

Erie County

The 3-acre Lake Front Park is located just west of the Huron River, lakeward of Wall and Park streets at the end of Ohio and Center streets. Free parking is available here.

The grass areas of the park are shaded by old-growth trees. Picnic tables, grills, playground equipment , gazebo, benches overlooking Lake Erie, restroom facilities and a drinking fountain are found in the upper park area. Grass leads down a gentle slope to the beach area which provides more than 615 feet of coastal access. The sand is mixed with shell fragments and a selection of stones and rocks perfect for skipping over the water.

Unless lake levels are high, the 445-foot detached breakwater is usually connected to the shore by the sand beach that ranges in from 90 feet wide on the west end to less than 20 feet wide on the east end. Fishing, walking and sunbathing atop the breakwater are common activities. Swimming is permitted and open water is accessible at both ends of the structure. The water level north of the park and south of the confined disposal facility is very shallow. During summer months, many local boaters anchor here. Kite board surfers and kayakers also use the park as a launch site.

A portion of the park east of Center Street and lakeward of Wall Street was acquired in part with a grant from the Ohio Coastal Management Program.

Lake Erie Public Access Guidebook

Field Notes:

_____

_____

_____

_____

_____

_____

_____

_____

_____

_____

_____

_____

_____

_____

_____

_____

_____

_____

_____

_____

_____

Amenities and Services:

Location Map:

N

Lake Erie

Lake Front Park

X

Huron Harbor West Pier

Cleveland

Wall

South

Ohio

Center

Williams

Main

Huron River

6

| 0 | 850 | 1,700 | 2,550 | 3,400 |

Feet

Erie

Date Visited: _____

Learn More:
City of Huron
Parks, Marina and Recreation
(419) 433-8487
www.cityofhuron.org

Huron Rotary Ce

Location:
Main and Wall streets
Huron, OH

Latitude:
N 41° 23.86'

Longitude:
W 082° 33.07'

Waterbody:
Lake Erie

Access Site Type:
Scenic

Environments:
Sandy Beach
Manmade Shore

Located at the terminus of North Main Street, the one-third acre Huron Rotary Centennial Park is on the west side of the entrance to the Huron Pier. The scenic, passive park overlooks Lake Erie affording distant views of Cedar Point and excellent sunsets year-round.

The park is denoted with a stone marker recognizing the Rotary Club's November 2006 dedication of the site. The park, along with Flemmond's Landing, another city park that is one block south overlooking the Huron River, are reminiscent of the city's maritime history, which included commercial fishing and shipbuilding.

Shipbuilding dates back to the early 1800s; by 1834, Huron was a major builder of wooden ships. Shipyards were located on the Huron River's west bank, slightly north of the park and upstream. Among the vessels built in Huron was the first lake ship to have above-deck cabins. When it was built in 1886, the ship *Golden Age* measured 286 feet and was the largest craft on the Great Lakes.

Huron shipbuilding declined as the nineteenth century drew to a close. Commercial fishing emerged thereafter, and served as Huron's economic cornerstone for more than fifty years. Huron's fishing enterprises declined in the 1950s when the waters, polluted at the time, could no longer support the commercial industry. Today, various marinas and charter boats are located upstream on the Huron River.

ntennial Park

Amenities and Services:

Field Notes:

_____

_____

_____

_____

_____

_____

_____

_____

_____

_____

_____

_____

_____

_____

_____

_____

Location Map:

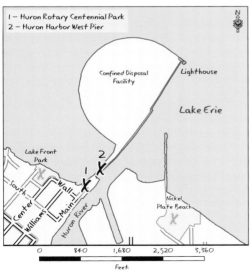

1 – Huron Rotary Centennial Park
2 – Huron Harbor West Pier

N

Confined Disposal Facility

Lighthouse

Lake Erie

Lake Front Park

2

1

South

Wall

Center

Williams

Main

Huron River

Nickel Plate Beach

0   840   1,680   2,520   3,360

Feet

Erie County

Date Visited: _____

Learn More:
City of Huron
Parks, Marina and Recreation
(419) 433-8487
www.cityofhuron.org

Huron Harbor We

Location:
Main and Wall streets
Huron, OH

Latitude:
N 41° 23.89'

Longitude:
W 082° 33.02'

Waterbody:
Lake Erie
Huron River

**Access
Site Type:**
Impervious
Pier

Environments:
Riparian/River
Manmade Shore

<vertical>Erie
County</vertical>

Located at the terminus of North Main Street on the west bank of the Huron River, the two-third mile long West Pier provides access to the Huron Lighthouse.

The West Pier is a jetty, which, along with the jetty on the east riverbank, helps keep the river's shipping channel open.

Constructed in 1939, the 72-foot-tall white steel tower, pyramidal lighthouse was one of the first electrically powered beacons on Lake Erie. The light was formerly operated by remote control from an on-shore brick station, but was automated in 1972. The light can be seen over a twelve-mile radius and is maintained by the United States Coast Guard.

The Huron Spoil Site, a confined disposal facility, is located along the northern two-thirds of the pier's west side. This approximately 68-acre containment facility may one day be a park; however, the site is currently only partially filled. The facility is owned by the U.S. Army Corps of Engineers.

The pier and the cement foundation surrounding the lighthouse are open year-round. Both are popular sites for fishing, walking and bird watching. The southern portion of the pier is handicap accessible. The northern extent is comprised of large limestone blocks of varying heights which require an able-footed walker to traverse. There are no other amenities on site.

Lake Erie Public Access Guidebook

+ Pier

Amenities and Services:

Location Map:

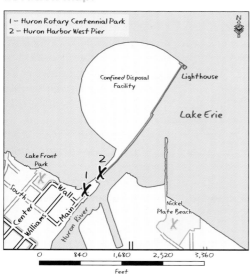

1 – Huron Rotary Centennial Park
2 – Huron Harbor West Pier

Confined Disposal Facility

Lighthouse

Lake Erie

Lake Front Park

Nickel Plate Beach

South
Center
Williams
Wall
Main
Huron River

| 0 | 840 | 1,680 | 2,520 | 3,360 |

Feet

Erie County

Field Notes:

Date Visited: _____

Learn More:
City of Huron
Parks, Marina and Recreation
(419) 433-8487
www.cityofhuron.org

Nickel Plate Beach

Location:
Nickel Plate Drive at Tiffin Avenue Huron, OH

Latitude:
N 41° 23.74′

Longitude:
W 082° 32.67′

Waterbody:
Lake Erie

Access Site Type:
Recreational

Environments:
Sandy Beach

Erie County's largest public swimming beach is located just east of the Huron River at the end of Nickel Plate Drive.

The 12.3-acre Nickel Plate Beach is comprised of natural sand containing only minor amounts of shell fragments and small stones – some of which are perfect for skipping. The very popular bathing and swimming beach has foot-friendly sand which extends into the water. The shallow nearshore includes an extensive sand-bar system. During certain wind and high-wave conditions, rip currents have occurred at this beach. (*see beach safety tips in the introduction*). However, at other times the water is calm.

The park grounds include a picnic shelter and tables, grills, benches, portable restrooms, three beach volleyball courts and playground equipment on the beach. There are no lifeguards on duty; life rings are located in the Beach Safety Box found at the base of the flag pole.

The Huron River's one-third mile east jetty is accessible from Nickel Plate Beach. The foot of the large limestone block jetty is within the wooded area on the beach's west side. A small pocket beach on the river, along with the jetty, both offer fishing access.

During summer, a daily parking fee is required for vehicles to park at the beach lot, or a seasonal pass can be purchased. The beach is open to foot and bicycle traffic year-round for free.

Erie County

Field Notes:

_____

_____

_____

_____

_____

_____

_____

_____

Amenities and Services:

Location Map:

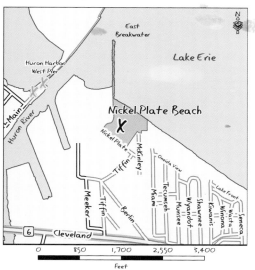

East Breakwater

Lake Erie

Huron Harbor
West Pier

Nickel Plate Beach

_____

_____

_____

_____

_____

_____

_____

_____

_____

_____

_____

Date Visited: _____

Learn More:
City of Huron
Parks, Marina and Recreation
(419) 433-8487
www.cityofhuron.org

Erie
County

Old Woman Creek S

Location:
U.S. Route 6 (Cleveland Road E), west of state Route 61
2514 Cleveland Road
Berlin Township , OH

Latitude:
N 41° 23.00'

Longitude:
W 082° 30.89'

Waterbody:
Lake Erie
Old Woman Creek

Access Site Type:
Educational
Natural

Environments:
Riparian/River
Estuarine
Sandy Beach
Wetland

Located 3 miles east of Huron, Old Woman Creek (OWC) National Estuarine Research Reserve is one of 27 coastal reserves connected nationally through the National Oceanic and Atmospheric Administration (NOAA) to address state and regional coastal management needs through research, education and stewardship.

The majority of the 574-acre preserve is located south of U.S. Route 6 (Cleveland Road) and surrounds the estuary. OWC is one of the state's few remaining examples of a natural Lake Erie estuary. Estuaries are transition zones where freshwater from an inland river is mixed with water from a Great Lake or ocean. Estuaries represent one of the most sensitive and ecologically important habitats on earth providing sanctuary for many plant and animal species.

OWC's habitats include wetlands, upland forests, open water, tributary streams, barrier beach and near shore Lake Erie. The preserve's 8 acres north of Cleveland Road provide coastal access and include a 760-foot beach and the creek mouth, which is sometimes separated from the open lake water by a naturally occurring sand bar.

The Mike DeWine Center for Coastal Wetland Studies is at the preserve; the center is a green building demonstration site. The Center provides ecological research laboratories and interpretative exhibits in the Visitors Center.

This preserve, located near the most southerly point on the Great Lakes, is managed as a cooperative partnership between NOAA and the ODNR Division of Wildlife. OWC is also an Ohio State Nature Preserve.

ate Nature Preserve
nd National Estuarine Research Reserve

Amenities and Services:

Field Notes:

_____

_____

_____

_____

_____

_____

_____

_____

_____

_____

_____

_____

_____

_____

_____

_____

_____

Location Map:

Lake Erie

Old Woman Creek
State Nature Preserve

Cleveland

Loon

Heron

W Old Lake

6

Visitor
Center

Old Woman Creek

Berlin

2

Darrow

| 0 | 1,600 | 3,200 | 4,800 | 6,400 |

Feet

Date Visited: _____

Learn More:
Old Woman Creek National Estuarine
Research Reserve
(419) 433-4601
www.oldwomancreek.org

Erie
County

Joppa and Risder

The 0.16-acre Joppa Road Access is at the road's northern terminus, 0.2 miles north of U.S. Route 6 in Vermilion Township on the road so named.

Three signs along a guardrail mark the end of the paved road and the beginning of the park. The steep, grass-covered slope down to Lake Erie is flanked by on the west by a green chain link fence and evergreen trees. At the slope's bottom, a narrow strip of uncut vegetation extends above a narrow beach comprised of various sizes of rocks and chunks of concrete. Driftwood – ranging from trees to small twigs – occasionally washes up on the beach.

Park signage denotes that the site is open from dawn to dusk. Swimming, at your own risk, is allowed; however, diving, ice fishing, walking and climbing on ice are prohibited. The park sign for the Joppa Road Access matches the sign at Vermilion Township's other end-of-road access site, Risden Road.

At the northern terminus of the Risden Road, the 0.14-acre park is one-tenth a mile north of U.S. Route 6 and about 2.4 miles east of the Joppa Road Access.

Signs and a guardrail also mark the end of the drivable road and the beginning of the park. The site is partially shaded by tress on a small, seasonally mowed grassy area. A variety of plants and small trees lead down the bluff face to Lake Erie.

Road Accesses

Erie County

Location Map (Joppa Road):

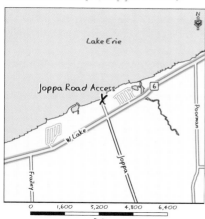

Lake Erie

Joppa Road Access

W Lake

Joppa

Poorman

Frailey

6

| 0 | 1,600 | 3,200 | 4,800 | 6,400 |

Feet

Location Map (Risden Road):

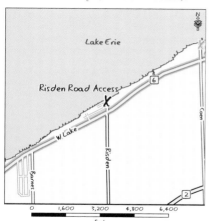

Lake Erie

Risden Road Access

W Lake

Barnes

Risden

Coen

6

2

| 0 | 1,600 | 3,200 | 4,800 | 6,400 |

Feet

Amenities and Services: (Joppa)

Amenities and Services: (Risden)

Field Notes:

_____

_____

_____

_____

_____

_____

_____

_____

_____

Date Visited: _____

Learn More:
Vermilion Township
(440) 967-3251
www.vermiliontownship.com

Coen Road Acces

Location:
End of Coen Road
Vermilion Township,
OH

Latitude:
N 41° 24.97′

Longitude:
W 082° 23.45′

Waterbody:
Lake Erie

**Access
Site Type:**
Scenic
Right-of-way

Environments:
Sandy Beach

Erie
County

The 0.21-acre Coen Road Access is located at the northern terminus of the road so named in Vermilion Township just north of the U.S. Route 6 (West Lake Road) intersection.

While small in size, the Coen Road Access, also known as the "Vermilion Township Memorial Gardens" is a hidden coastal treasure with a whimsical feel that leaves a lasting impression.

Behind an arbor signed "Welcome to the Garden" a faux lighthouse greets visitors to a collection of planted flower beds, monuments, sitting places, water features and nautical memorabilia. A variety of pavers – ranging from natural limestone to pressed concrete – create an eclectic winding staircase/path that leads down through the garden down to a seemingly secret, quiet beach area.

Parking for the Coen Road Access is available at Sherod Park, which is adjacent to the east.

Field Notes:

_____

_____

_____

_____

_____

_____

_____

_____

Amenities and Services:

Location Map:

_____

_____

_____

_____

_____

_____

_____

_____

_____

_____

Date Visited: _____

Learn More:
Vermilion Township
(440) 967-3251
www.vermiliontownship.com

Sherod Park

Location:
U.S. Route 6 and
Coen Road
Vermilion Township, OH

Latitude:
N 41° 24.92'

Longitude:
W 082° 23.39'

Waterbody:
Lake Erie

**Access
Site Type:**
Recreational

Environments:
Bluff
Riparian/River
Sandy Beach

Erie County

The 21.2-acre Sherod Park in Vermilion Township is located northeast of the Coen Road and U.S. Route 6 (West Lake Road) intersection. Sherod Park is adjacent to the west of the Coen Road Access, a 0.21-acre end-of-road access site. Combined, the two sites create nearly a quarter mile of coastal access on Lake Erie.

Atop a low, graded, vegetated bluff, a line of park benches spaced between deciduous trees affords scenic views of Lake Erie. One of the park's parking lots is located just south of the grassy area at the top of the bluff, allowing those who wish to sit in their vehicles equally scenic views.

The Sherod Park beach is predominately sand; however, groins along the beach have accumulated larger quantities of invasive shells and rocks near the water's edge. The vegetated groins also provide Lake Erie fishing access.

Sherod Park's amenities include monuments, baseball and soccer fields, playground equipment, a picnic pavilion and a Par Course Fit Center exercise trail.

An Ohio Coastal Management Program grant funded, in part, the *Sherod Park Development Study – Feasibility Project* in 1998.

Field Notes:

_____

_____

_____

_____

_____

_____

_____

_____

_____

_____

_____

_____

_____

_____

_____

_____

_____

_____

_____

_____

_____

Amenities and Services:

Location Map:

Lake Erie

Coen Road Access
"Vermilion Township
Memorial Gardens"

Sherod Park

6

W Lake

Coen

| 0 | 850 | 1,700 | 2,550 | 3,400 |

Feet

Erie
County

Date Visited: _____

Learn More:
City of Vermilion
Recreation Department
(440) 204-2490
www.cityofvermilion.com

Main Street Beach

Location:
End of Main Street
Vermilion, OH

Latitude:
N 41° 25.50'

Longitude:
W 082° 21.97'

Waterbody:
Lake Erie

**Access
Site Type:**
Recreational

Environments:
Sandy Beach

At just under one acre and 300 feet of lake frontage, Main Street Beach is a small, popular Lake Erie swimming beach in downtown Vermilion. The natural sand beach is located adjacent to the east of the Great Lakes Historical Society's Inland Seas Maritime Museum.

The Great Lakes Historical Society is a nonprofit organization dedicated to the preservation of Great Lakes history. Its Inland Seas Maritime Museum contains one of the world's largest collections of Great Lakes historical maritime artifacts, documents, ship models, and original artwork. A replica of the original Vermilion Lighthouse sits on the museum's property.

The lighthouse, Lake Erie and the pleasure boats entering and exiting the mouth of the Vermilion River can be seen from Main Street Beach. At the back of the beach, a large handicap accessible observation deck affords these views. The site has few other amenities.

Parking is available on Main Street north of U.S. Route 6 (Liberty Avenue) and south of the beach.

Field Notes:

Amenities and Services:

Location Map:

Lake Erie

Main Street Beach

Erie County

Date Visited: _____

Learn More:
City of Vermilion
Recreation Department
(440) 204-2490
www.cityofvermilion.com

North Shore Alvar S:

Location:
Division Street and
Titus Road (SR 575)
920 Division Street
Kelleys Island, OH

Latitude:
N 41° 37.21'

Longitude:
W 082° 42.67'

Waterbody:
Lake Erie

**Access
Site Type:**
Natural

Environments:
Bluff

The 3.8-acre North Shore Alvar State Nature Preserve on Kelleys Island is home to Ohio's finest and most intact alvar community.

Alvars are uncommon, yet distinct land features characterized by exposed limestone or dolostone bedrock, thin soils with high pH levels and sparse vegetation. Due to minimal soil and tree cover, alvars are subject to drought, flooding and extreme temperatures and have distinct plant communities adapted to such conditions. Lake Erie's Western Basin is the only place in Ohio where alvars are found. Almost all of North America's alvars occur within the Great Lakes basin. Although some 120 alvars exist in the Great Lakes, they comprise only 0.2 percent of the land.

Only a few specially adapted plant species survive in the North Shore Alvar including the northern bog violet (an endangered species), balsam squaw-weed, Kalm's lobelia, Pringle's aster and the rare showy orange lichen (shown in the far-left photo above). It is believed that the limestone cliffs of the Lake Erie islands are the only places in Ohio where this lichen is found.

North Shore Alvar Nature Preserve is located within Kelleys Island State Park on the north side of the island and is accessible via the North Shore Loop trail. Portions of the alvar are smooth, flat and easy to traverse; other sections are narrow, near the bluff face and one must be more sure-footed navigate.

te Nature Preserve

Amenities and Services:

Field Notes:

Location Map:

Lake Erie

North Shore Alvar
State Nature Preserve
X

Glacial
Grooves

575

Kelleys Island
State Park
X

Titus

Division

| 0 | 1,000 | 2,000 | 3,000 | 4,000 |

Feet

Erie County

Date Visited: _____

Learn More:
ODNR Division of
Natural Areas and Preserves
ohiodnr.com/dnap
ohiodnr.com/tabid/916/default.aspx

Kelleys Island State

Location:
Division Street and
Titus Road (SR 575)
Kelleys Island, OH

Latitude:
N 41° 36.86'

Longitude:
W 082° 42.37'

Waterbody:
Lake Erie

**Access
Site Type:**
Recreational

Environments:
Bluff
Sandy Beach

The 677-acre Kelleys Island State Park provides nearly a mile of coastal access on Kelleys Island. The park's office and campgrounds are located on a park road off of Division Street just south of the Titus Road (State Route 575) intersection. Division Street extends north to the park from downtown Kelleys Island.

The park includes a natural sand swimming beach that occupies the northwest cove on the north side of the island. Compared to some mainland beaches, the turbidity of the water north of Kelleys Island is very clear because there are no Lake Erie tributaries contributing sediment to the nearshore water.

Kelleys Island State Park features many recreational amenities, including 125 camp sites, two seasonal Rent-A-Yurts, a group camp area, a picnic pavilion and tables, a boat launch and trails where mountain biking is permitted. A pier near the boat launch is accessible for fishing as are other waterside locations. Hunting is permissible during the appropriate seasons.

Kelleys Island State Park is the only state park located in Erie County.

Both the North Shore Alvar and North Pond state nature preserves are accessible from the state park. The Kelleys Island Glacial Grooves State Memorial is located within the park at the northwest corner of Division Street and Titus Road.

Park

Amenities and Services:

Location Map:

Field Notes:

Date Visited: _____

Learn More:
ODNR Division of Parks and Recreation
Kelleys Island State Park
(419) 746-2546 – seasonally
ohiodnr.com/parks
ohiodnr.com/tabid/753/default.aspx

North Pond State

Location:
Ward-Hamilton Road,
east of Division Street
Kelleys Island, OH

Latitude:
N 41° 36.43'

Longitude:
W 082° 41.96'

Waterbody:
Lake Erie

**Access
Site Type:**
Natural

Environments:
Sandy Beach
Wetland

The 45-acre North Pond State Nature Preserve is a nearly pristine wetland with a channel leading to Lake Erie in Kelleys Island's North Bay. The preserve was dedicated in October 1999.

The sanctuary is Ohio's only state-managed, lake embayment natural pond. Water levels in embayment ponds, which occur along the Great Lakes' coasts, rise and fall with that of the lakes. These ponds formed as the lakes receded from their ancient shores. At one time, Ohio's islands had 12 embayment ponds. North Pond is the most intact of the three remaining. The others are on Middle Bass and North Bass islands in Ottawa County.

North Pond is also one of the few remaining natural wetlands directly connected to Lake Erie. Most have been impounded by dikes, which artificially control water levels. North Pond's aquatic ecosystem harbors a fascinating assemblage of plant and animal life, much of which may be viewed from the one-mile recycled plastic lumber boardwalk that winds through the preserve and leads to the beach. The site also includes a raised observation deck.

Vegetation in the pond and surrounding swamp forest varies depending on the pond's water level. The area is known for the tremendous numbers of waterfowl migrating through in the spring and fall. During these seasons, numerous species of ducks and other water bird will be seen.

Nature Preserve

Amenities and Services:

Field Notes:

_____

_____

_____

_____

_____

_____

_____

_____

_____

_____

_____

_____

_____

_____

_____

_____

Location Map:

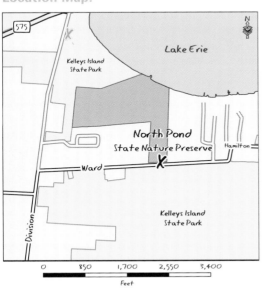

575

Lake Erie

Kelleys Island
State Park

North Pond
State Nature Preserve

Hamilton

Ward

X

Division

Kelleys Island
State Park

N

0   850   1,700   2,550   3,400

Feet

Erie
County

Date Visited: _____

Learn More:
ODNR Division of
Natural Areas and Preserves
ohiodnr.com/dnap
ohiodnr.com/tabid/952/Default.aspx

Inscription Rock St

Location:
East Lake Shore Drive,
near Addison Avenue
Kelleys Island, OH

Latitude:
N 41° 35.57'

Longitude:
W 082° 42.41'

Waterbody:
Lake Erie

**Access
Site Type:**
Cultural

Environments:
Sandy Beach

The quarter-acre Inscription Rock is one of Ohio's most famous rock art sites. Listed on the National Register of Historic Places, Inscription Rock is on Kelleys Island's south side just east of downtown.

The 32-foot by 21-foot rock surface is covered with one of the finest examples of aboriginal art in the Great Lakes region. Known as "petroglyphs" from the Greek words for rock writing, no one is sure what the unusual drawings depict. The most widely accepted theory is that the large rock was used as a "message stone" where various Native Americans would make drawings noting travels and important achievements.

The precise age of Inscription Rock's carvings is unknown. Based on the symbolism and the amount of weathering of the limestone, historians believe the drawings are probably less than 1,000 years old, and likely the work of the Late Prehistoric period inhabitants. There was once another boulder with petroglyphs along the north side of Kelleys Island, but limestone quarry workers blasted it apart in the mid-1800s.

Inscription Rock's markings have been greatly eroded by exposure to the weather; today it is difficult to see them. In 1969 the Ohio Historical Society erected a cover and viewing platform to preserve the rock. A small-portion plaster replica of the accurate and detailed sketches done in the 1850s is at the site.

There are no recreational amenities at this site.

ate Memorial

Amenities and Services:

Location Map:

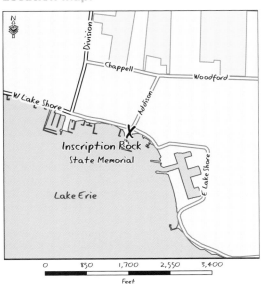

Division
Chappell
Woodford
W Lake Shore
Addison
Inscription Rock
State Memorial
E Lake Shore
Lake Erie

N

| 0 | 850 | 1,700 | 2,550 | 3,400 |

Feet

Field Notes:

_____
_____
_____
_____
_____
_____
_____
_____
_____
_____
_____
_____
_____
_____

Date Visited: _____

Learn More:
Ohio Historical Society
www.ohiohistory.org

Hancock-Wood Ele

Erie
County

The half-acre Hancock-Wood Electric Scenic Overlook area welcomes visitors to Kelleys Island with a sign proclaiming such. The overlook is located on the south side of West Lake Shore Drive (State Route 575) just west of the downtown.

The overlook is a few hundred yards east of where the former Neuman Ferry & Cruise Line docked. Passengers used to pass the overlook as they walked east into the village. In 2002, the nearly 100-year-old company was bought by its competitor, the Kelleys Island Ferry. This ferry service docks southeast of the village and is the only auto-passenger ferry providing daily service to the island. The Jet Express and the Goodtime I ferry services provide seasonal passenger-only service to Kelleys Island and dock downtown.

Shaded by an old-growth tree, amenities at Hancock-Wood Electric Scenic Overlook include a picnic table, observation deck, binoculars and park benches looking south out over Lake Erie water toward the mainland of the Marblehead Peninsula.

This scenic overlook is owned by the Hancock-Wood Electric Cooperative.

...ric Scenic Overlook

Amenities and Services:

Location Map:

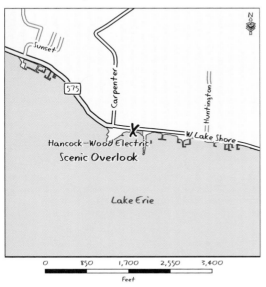

Sunset

Carpenter

575

Huntington

W Lake Shore

✗

Hancock—Wood Electric
Scenic Overlook

Lake Erie

N

| 0 | 850 | 1,700 | 2,550 | 3,400 |

Feet

Field Notes:

_____

_____

_____

_____

_____

_____

_____

_____

_____

_____

_____

_____

_____

_____

_____

_____

Date Visited: _____

Learn More:
Hancock-Wood Electric
Cooperative, Inc.
(419) 746-2533

Established: December 26, 1822
2000 Population: 284,664
2010 Projection: 290,840
Land Area and Rank: 492.6 square miles, 29 of 88
County Seat: City of Elyria
Named for: French Province of Lorraine

Miles of Coast: 23 miles
Miles of Publicly Accessible Coast: 2.1 miles
Number of Access Sites: 15

Lorain County

A brief history:

Lorain County was formed December 26, 1822, from portions of Huron, Medina and Cuyahoga counties which were originally part of the Connecticut Western Reserve. The county's 493 square miles were settled by people attracted to jobs in industries such as shipbuilding, steelmaking and fishing.

In the later part of the 20th century, the county's population grew dramatically. Residents of nearby Cleveland in Cuyahoga County moved west to Lorain and surrounding counties. However, today Lorain County is still overwhelmingly rural, with only seven percent of the county deemed to be urban. Most residents earn their living by working in manufacturing, sales or service positions. Farming ranks eighth. Some county residents also earn their living on Lake Erie.

Elyria is the county seat and the second largest community in the county. The coastal city of Lorain is the largest.

The county is named for the Lorraine region of France. Many of the county's earliest European settlers were abolitionists. Oberlin College, in the city so named, was the first institution of higher education in the United States to admit women and African Americans into the same classes as white men.

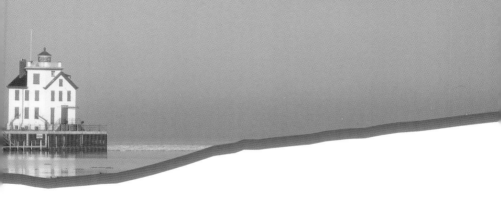

Learn More:

Lorain County
www.loraincounty.us

City of Avon Lake
www.avonlake.org

City of Lorain
www.cityoflorain.org

City of Sheffield Lake
www.sheffieldlake.net

City of Vermilion
www.vermilion.net

Lorain County Chamber of Commerce
www.loraincountychamber.com

Lorain County Metro Parks
www.metroparks.cc

Lorain County Visitors Bureau
www.visitloraincounty.com

North Coast Regional Chamber of Commerce
www.northcoastchamber.com

Vermilion Chamber of Commerce
www.vermilionohio.com

Public Access Management:

Local	13
Local/Metropark	1
Port Authority	1

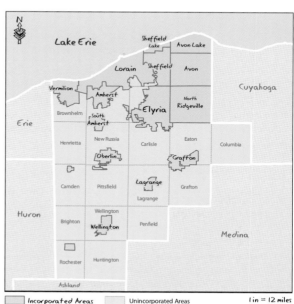

Showse Park

Location:
Edgewater Drive at
Claremont Road
Vermilion, OH

Latitude:
N 41° 25.78'

Longitude:
W 082° 18.84'

Waterbody:
Lake Erie

**Access
Site Type:**
Recreational

Environments:
Bluff
Sandy Beach

Lorain
County

The 18.5-acre Showse Park is situated both north and south of Edgewater Drive in the city of Vermilion about three miles east of downtown. Showse Park is also an access point along the Vermilion-Lorain Water Trail. The park's name, "Showse" is an acronym representing original north coast inhabitants- Native American tribes including the Sandusky, Huron, Ottawa, Wyandot, Seneca and Erie.

The park's northern portion provides Lake Erie access. Benches line the top of the clay bluff on the partially shaded, mowed grass area north of the road. A mulch-covered walking trail extends around the perimeter of the park and parallels the shore for much of the park's width.

A dirt-gravel access trail descends the bluff face from the middle of the lot, down to the beach – a mixture of sand and small stones. A groin made of large concrete blocks extends 50 feet into Lake Erie providing fishing access in addition to that found along the approximate 525-foot shore. Signs posted atop the bluff warn that there is no lifeguard and swimming is at one's own risk.

Showse Park's southern extent includes most of the park's amenities. The park's main parking lots are accessible off Edgewater Drive. Additional access and limited parking is at the terminus of Berkley Road east of the Claremont Road intersection. The *2000 Showse Park Feasibility Study* was funded, in part, by an Ohio Coastal Management Program grant.

Field Notes:

_____

_____

_____

_____

_____

_____

_____

_____

_____

_____

Amenities and Services:

Location Map:

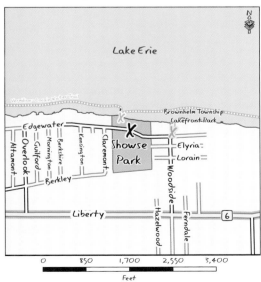

Date Visited: _____

Learn More:
City of Vermilion
Recreation Department
(440) 204 2490
www.vermilion.net

Brownhelm Town

Location:
Edgewater Drive at
Woodside Avenue
Vermilion, OH

Latitude:
N 41° 25.76'

Longitude:
W 082° 18.62'

Waterbody:
Lake Erie

**Access
Site Type:**
Scenic

Environments:
Bluff
Rocky Shore
Sandy Beach

Lorain County

The nearly half-acre Brownhelm Township Lakefront Park is a township-managed park located within the Vermilion city limits. Located less than one-tenth a mile east of Showse Park, Brownhelm Township Lakefront Park is at the north terminus of Woodside Avenue north of the Edgewater Drive intersection.

Deciduous trees line the eastern side of this pocket of mowed grass green space. Adjacent to the road is a small gravel parking lot and signage recognizing the park. A picnic table made of recycled plastic and benches looking north over Lake Erie are the park's only amenities.

The less-than 100-foot shore is a small pocket beach of sand heavily mixed with shell fragments and small stones. Swimming and fishing from shore are allowed; however, there is no visible path down the steep, heavily vegetated bluff that is signed, "Caution. Hazardous area. Use at your own risk."

The park is open from dawn to dusk. Alcoholic beverages are prohibited; dogs must be controlled by hand held leashes.

‎ip Lakefront

Amenities and Services:

Location Map:

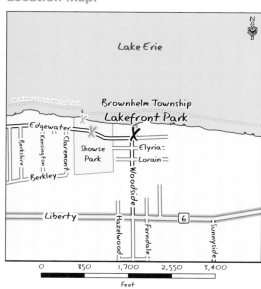

Lake Erie

Vermilion Coastal Wa-Pee Trail

Brownhelm Township
Lakefront Park

Edgewater

Berkshire
Kensington
Claremont

Showse
Park

Elyria
Lorain

Berkley

Woodside

Liberty

Hazelwood
Ferndale
Sunnyside

6

| 0 | 850 | 1,700 | 2,550 | 3,400 |

Feet

Lorain County

Field Notes:

_____
_____
_____
_____
_____
_____
_____
_____
_____
_____
_____
_____
_____
_____
_____
_____

Date Visited: _____

Learn More:
Brownhelm Township
Parks and Recreation
(440) 984-2243
cpmra.muohio.edu/townships/brown-
helm

Waverly Place Park

Location:
End of Waverly
Place Drive
Lorain, OH

Latitude:
N 41° 27.70'

Longitude:
W 082° 11.98'

Waterbody:
Lake Erie

**Access
Site Type:**
Scenic
Right-of-Way

Environments:
Bluff

Lorain County

The 0.57-acre Waverly Place Park is at the northern terminus of the Waverly Place cul-de-sac, which is north of U.S. Route 6 (West Erie Avenue) in the city of Lorain.

This small patch of well-shaded green space has no recreational amenities and limited parking at the end of the street. There is no signage recognizing the park, which is seamlessly connected to the west of the adjacent and much larger Lakeview Park.

The very steep glacial till bluff leading down to Lake Erie's shore is partially vegetated. A steel staircase guides foot traffic down the center of a bluff to a steel landing. The shore is mostly comprised of large rocks and concrete rubble.

Amenities and Services:

Location Map:

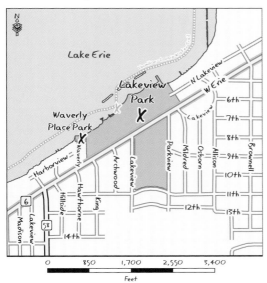

Lorain

Date Visited: _____

Learn More:
City of Lorain
Parks and Recreation
(440) 244-9000
www.cityoflorain.org

Lakeview Park

Location:
West Erie (US 6) and
Parkview avenues
Lorain, OH

Latitude:
N 41° 27.78'

Longitude:
W 082° 11.72'

Waterbody:
Lake Erie

**Access
Site Type:**
Recreational

Environments:
Bluff
Sandy Beach

Lorain
County

The expansive 42.3-acre Lakeview Park is on U.S. Route 6 (West Erie Avenue) one mile west of the Black River in the city of Lorain. Parkland is on both sides of the road with the northern 20 acres providing access to Lake Erie. Lakeview Park is also an access point along the Vermilion-Lorain Water Trail.

Lakeview Park includes a one-third mile groomed swimming beach. The foot-friendly sand is darker than many Ohio beaches because 110,000 cubic yards of sand from an upland source was placed here in 1977 when the three breakwaters were constructed. The breakwaters, a large groin at the beach's east end, and two smaller groins at the beach's western extent stabilize the beach and provide fishing access. During summer months, lifeguards are on duty daily from noon to 6 pm.

In 2007, Lakeview's beach area was transformed. The bluff was re-graded to allow for handicap accessible sidewalks leading down to the beach. A new bathhouse was constructed in the design of the original 1920s building. The bathhouse contains a café and eight family changing rooms (five with showers).

Playground equipment and volleyball courts are located on the beach and in upper areas of the park; amenities also include picnic shelters and tables, paved trails, the Historic Rose Garden, lawn bowling, two amphitheaters, spectacular sunsets and views of the Lorain Lighthouse. Parking is located north of U.S. Route 6 which, shares its path with the Back Roads & Beaches Bike Trail through Lorain County.

Field Notes:

_____

_____

_____

_____

Amenities and Services:

_____

_____

_____

_____

_____

_____

_____

_____

_____

_____

_____

Location Map:

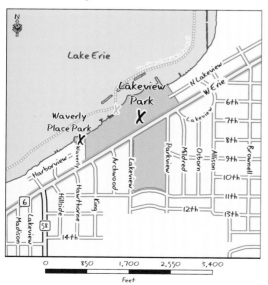

_____

_____

_____

_____

_____

_____

Date Visited: _____

Learn More:
Lorain County Metro Parks
www.metroparks.cc
and
City of Lorain - Parks and Recreation
(440) 244-9000
www.cityoflorain.org

City of Lorain Public

Location:
First Street at
Oberlin Avenue
Lorain, OH

Latitude:
N 41° 28.24'

Longitude:
W 082° 11.12'

Waterbody:
Lake Erie

**Access
Site Type:**
Impervious
Pier

Environments:
Manmade Shore

The city of Lorain's nearly 2-acre Public Boat Ramp provides six ramps and three parking lots for direct Lake Erie boating access. Entrance to the site is north of the Oberlin Avenue and First Street intersection with one-way traffic directed to exit on the drive and parking lot along First Street near the Hamilton Avenue intersection.

This site is Lorain's oldest boat launch and is locally known as "Hot Waters" because of its location between a power plant's warm water discharge on the west and the former ore docks to the east (now the Lorain Public Fishing Pier access site).

Three of the boat ramps are dedicated for launching vessels up to 24 feet long and three are dedicated for boat recovery. Launching of personal watercraft is allowed but may be restricted to the shallowest launch lane on busy days. Boaters are reminded to follow the 100-yard "No Wake" zone which extends from the end of the pier into Lorain Harbor.

Fishing access is provided around the perimeter of the on-water asphalt parking lot which has car-trailer and car-only parking. A second gravel lot is just east of the launch ramps and a third asphalt lot is about 100 yards south of the launch.

The public boat ramp is a city of Lorain Adopt-a-Spot location adopted by the Polish Fisherman's Club. The site includes a bait and tackle store which also sells ice and some food items.

Lake Erie Public Access Guidebook

Boat Ramp

Amenities and Services:

Location Map:

1 – City of Lorain Public Boat Ramp
2 – City of Lorain Public Fishing Pier

Lake Erie

N

Lakeside Landing

Lakeside

Black River

1 X   2 X

6

Black River Landing

1st
2nd
W Erie
4th
5th
6th
7th

57

N Lakeview

Lakeview

Oberlin

Hamilton

Washington

Reid

Broadway

0   1,000   2,000   3,000   4,000

Feet

Field Notes:

_____
_____
_____
_____
_____
_____
_____
_____
_____
_____
_____
_____
_____
_____
_____
_____
_____
_____
_____

Date Visited: _____

Learn More:
City of Lorain
Parks and Recreation
(440) 244-9000
www.cityoflorain.org

Lorain County

City of Lorain Public

Location:
First Street at
Hamilton Avenue
Lorain, OH

Latitude:
N 41° 28.25'

Longitude:
W 082° 11.00'

Waterbody:
Lake Erie
Black River

**Access
Site Type:**
Impervious
Pier

Environments:
Riparian/River
Manmade Shore

The city of Lorain's 25.5-acre Public Fishing Pier provides access to the Black River and Lake Erie inside the Lorain Harbor.

Surrounded by a green fence, three unmarked openings provide pier access. Two entrances are north of 1st Street, just west of, and at the Washington Avenue intersection. The third entrance is off Black River Lane just east of the Broadway Street intersection. All entrances are north of U.S. Route 6.

The public fishing access starts near the foot of the 1,052-foot Charles Berry Bridge which spans the Black River. The bridge is the largest double-leaf bascule-style bridge in the United States. From the bridge, a paved concrete handicap-accessible bulkhead used for fishing and walking extends for more than a half-mile along the river, north into Lorain Harbor.

The land west of the bulkhead is divided into three distinct sections. The southern third is covered in gravel and painted with lines to aid in parking. At times, city of Lorain vehicles including police cruisers are parked here. Vehicles are permitted to drive to the pier's northern extent which is mostly well-packed dirt. The north section is split by a ship slip; fishing is allowed along both sides.

The pier's mid-section is being overtaken by wetland and grasses, a stark contrast to the pier's industrial past as the former site of Lorain's Hulett Automatic Ore Unloaders and iron ore piles.

Fishing Pier

Amenities and Services:

Location Map:

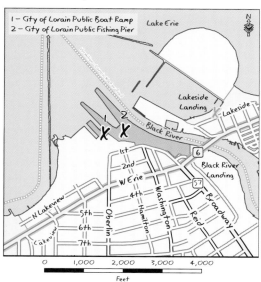

1 – City of Lorain Public Boat Ramp
2 – City of Lorain Public Fishing Pier

Lake Erie

Lakeside Landing

Lakeside

Black River

Black River Landing

1st
2nd
W Erie
4th
5th
6th
7th

N Lakeview
Lakeview
Oberlin
Hamilton
Washington
Reid
Broadway

6
57

0   1,000   2,000   3,000   4,000
Feet

Field Notes:

_____
_____
_____
_____
_____
_____
_____
_____
_____
_____
_____
_____
_____
_____
_____
_____
_____
_____

Date Visited: _____

Learn More:
City of Lorain
Parks & Recreation Department
(440) 244-9000
www.cityoflorain.org

Lorain County

Lakeside Landing

Location:
Lakeside and
Colorado avenues
Lorain, OH

Latitude:
N 41° 28.33′

Longitude:
W 082° 10.5′

Waterbody:
Lake Erie

**Access
Site Type:**
Recreational

Environments:
Rocky Shore
Sandy Beach
Manmade Shore

Lorain
County

The nearly 15-acre Lakeside Landing includes a small beach, a large pier, a scenic picnic overlook and a boat launch along 0.32 miles of shore north of Lakeside Avenue and just east of the Black River. From U.S. Route 6, the site's main parking lot is north of the Colorado Avenue intersection.

A small Lake Erie tributary crosses the east end of the site's 200-foot, non-swimming beach. The beach is comprised of large-grain sand and extends northeast to a stone revetment. The structure is near the south end of the 58-acre, D-shaped confined disposal facility (CDF) maintained by the U.S. Army Corps of Engineers. In 2010, 5.26 acres of the CDF were transferred to the Lorain Port Authority to become part of the Lakeside Landing access.

The Landing's large parking areas are south of the CDF. A 0.46–mile handicap-accessible concrete-paved pathway and wooden boardwalk extend the length of the CDF's west side out into Lake Erie. The pier allows for views of the Lorain Lighthouse. Fishing is permitted from the boardwalk and an 800-foot pier which extends east of the main boardwalk and north of the private marina docks. The docks are accessed via gates form the public boardwalk.

The Lorain Port Authority's Eastside Boat Launch is at the Landing's west side. A launch fee is charged. Two picnic pavilions and a privately owned restaurant are on site. Lakeside Landing is adjacent to the east of the U.S. Coast Guard Station Lorain and the Lorain Port Authority's Riverside Park which has playground equipment.

PARK RULES

Amenities and Services:

Location Map:

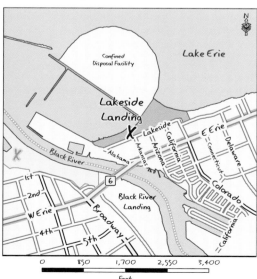

Field Notes:

Date Visited: _____

Learn More:
Lorain Port Authority
(440) 204-2269
www.lorainportauthority.com

Lorain County

Century Park

Location:
East Erie (US 6) and
Massachusetts avenues
Lorain, OH

Latitude:
N 41° 28.64′

Longitude:
W 082° 09.21′

Waterbody:
Lake Erie

**Access
Site Type:**
Recreational

Environments:
Bluff
Sandy Beach

Lorain
County

The 2.76-acre Century Park is 1.1 miles east of the Black River mouth and the city of Lorain's easternmost coastal recreation access location. Century's parking lot entrance is on U.S. Route 6 (East Erie Ave) just west of the Massachusetts Avenue intersection.

Century Park features a 320 foot long, large-grain, groomed sand beach mixed with small amounts of shell fragments and rocks. The beach's 75-foot width is protected on each end by a 150 foot long rock groin. These, along with a third poured concrete groin that bisects the beach, extend into Lake Erie providing fishing access.

A grass-covered bluff leads from the well-shaded upper park to the beach. Steps lead down the bluff's center while a graded, gravel path is at the park's eastern end.

Century Park is home to the Harbor House which among other events, houses Santa Claus and his helpers at their workshop during the Christmas season. Park amenities also include picnic tables, playground equipment and restroom facilities. Century Park is on the Back Roads & Beaches Bike Trail, which follows U.S. Route 6 through Lorain County. While not on contiguous property, Lorain's 32-acre Longfellow Park is one block to the south.

Field Notes:

_____

_____

_____

_____

_____

_____

_____

_____

_____

_____

_____

_____

_____

_____

_____

_____

_____

_____

_____

Amenities and Services:

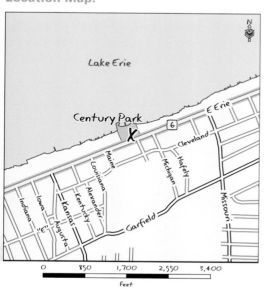

Location Map:

Lake Erie

Century Park

E Erie

6

Cleveland

Maine

Louisiana

Michigan

Hafely

Alexander

Kentucky

Missouri

Indiana

Iowa

Kansas

Augusta

"E"

Garfield

N

0   850   1,700   2,550   3,400

Feet

Lorain County

Date Visited: _____

Learn More:
City of Lorain
Parks and Recreation
(440) 244-9000
www.cityoflorain.org

Lakewood Beach

Location:
3801 Lake Road
and Lakewood
Beach Drive
Sheffield Lake, OH

Latitude:
N 41° 29.21′

Longitude:
W 082° 07.36′

Waterbody:
Lake Erie

**Access
Site Type:**
Recreational

Environments:
Sandy Beach

Lorain
County

The 0.7-acre Lakewood Beach Park on U.S. Route 6 (Lake Road) is the city of Sheffield Lake's westernmost public coastal access site. Lakewood Beach's asphalt parking lot is marked about 100 feet west of the Lakewood Beach Drive intersection. A white fence separates the parkland from the adjoining apartment complex.

Tall deciduous trees flank both sides of a dirt-sand path, which leads from the parking lot north to the beach. The path is marked on the west by a split-rail wood fence. A shaded picnic table and grill are placed near the conflux of the path with the open-sun beach area.

The beach is predominately sand, with small stones and shell fragments mixed in the sand near the shore. A small stream of water flows across the beach on the west side. Beach signage notes that no lifeguard is on duty and swimming should be done at one's own risk.

Lakewood Beach Park, open daily from dawn to dusk, is along the Back Roads & Beaches Bike Trail, which follows U.S. Route 6 in Lorain County. Bike racks are located at the park.

Park

Amenities and Services:

Location Map:

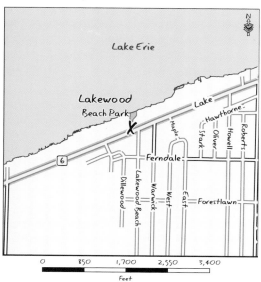

Field Notes:

_____
_____
_____
_____
_____
_____
_____
_____
_____
_____
_____
_____
_____
_____
_____
_____
_____
_____
_____
_____
_____

Date Visited: _____

Learn More:
City of Sheffield Lake
Parks and Recreation Department
(440) 949-5295
www.sheffieldlake.net

Lorain County

Sheffield Lake C

Location:
Lake Road (US 6) at
Lake Breeze Road
Sheffield Lake, OH

Latitude:
N 41° 29.39′

Longitude:
W 082° 06.79′

Waterbody:
Lake Erie

Access Site Type:
Recreational

Environments:
Sandy Beach
Manmade Shore

The 2.8-acre Sheffield Lake Community Park is on U.S. Route 6 (Lake Road) in the city of Sheffield Lake at the northwest terminus of Lake Breeze Road. The park is adjacent to the west of Sheffield Lake's Domonkas Branch Public Library. Beginning in 2007, the city received $865,000 in grants from the ODNR divisions of Wildlife and Watercraft for major park renovations that improved boating access.

A handicap accessible fishing pier in a large "L" shape protects the park's new two-lane boat launch for small craft (up to 30 feet). Overnight public parking for cars and trailers is available at the park as well as in the city-owned plaza on the south side of U.S. Route 6.

The pier, along with additional shore structures to the west, provides fishing access. The park's upper mowed-grass area includes picnic tables overlooking Lake Erie. Fronting this area is a handicap accessible paved concrete boardwalk that extends from the west side of the boat launch to the western edge of the park property.

The park's foot-friendly sand beach extends east of the fishing pier along Lake Erie. There are no lifeguards on duty; swimming at one's own risk is allowed.

Community Park's parking lot includes two small wind turbines. The park is along the Back Roads & Beaches Bike Trail, which follows U.S. Route 6 in Lorain County.

mmunity Park

Amenities and Services:

Location Map:

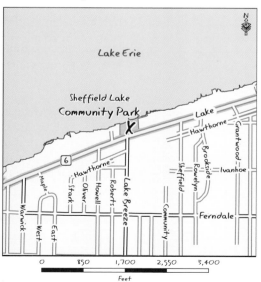

Lake Erie

Sheffield Lake
Community Park

0   850   1,700   2,550   3,400
Feet

Field Notes:

_____
_____
_____
_____
_____
_____
_____
_____
_____
_____
_____
_____
_____
_____
_____
_____
_____

Date Visited: _____

Learn More:
City of Sheffield Lake
Parks and Recreation Department
(440) 949-5295
www.sheffieldlake.net

West Shore Park

Location:
Lake Road (US 6)
between Sunset Ave
and West Shore Blvd
Sheffield Lake, OH

Latitude:
N 41° 29.62'

Longitude:
W 082° 05.91'

Waterbody:
Lake Erie

**Access
Site Type:**
Recreational

Environments:
Sandy Beach
Manmade Shore

Lorain County

The 2.8-acre West Shore Park on U.S. Route 6 (East Lake Road) is home to the Sheffield Lake Community Civic Center. The park spans both the south and north side of the road with coastal access provided on the north side.

West Shore Park's parking lot north of U.S. Route 6 with entrances about 250 feet east of Sunset Avenue and about 100 feet west of West Shore Boulevard. West Shore Park's east parking area is also accessible from the west end of the 4600 block of Edgewater Drive. An access road allows car traffic to drive around the north side of the civic center for scenic Lake Erie views.

Park amenities include playground equipment, a picnic shelter and tables, a gazebo and a small beach. A partially vegetated bluff leads from the upper mowed-grass area down to the shore. Portions of bluff face, along with portions of the shore, consist of large chunks of concrete armoring. The beach's width and length vary with water levels. The beach's sand is mixed with shells and shell fragments.

Similar to other Lorain County parks located on U.S. Route 6, this site is on the Back Roads & Beaches Bike Trail.

Field Notes:

Amenities and Services:

Location Map:

Lake Erie

West Shore Park

Lake

Edgewater

6

Hawthorne

Tennyson

Grantwood

Idlewood

Kenilworth

Hollywood

Pasadena

Sunset

Alameda

Oakwood

West Shore

Maplewood

Robinwood

Ivanhoe

Richelieu

Harris

Lafayette

Treadway

| 0 | 850 | 1,700 | 2,550 | 3,400 |

Feet

Date Visited: _____

Learn More:
City of Sheffield Lake
Parks and Recreation Department
(440) 949-5295
www.sheffieldlake.net

Lorain County

Jay Terrell's "Terrible Fish" The Dunkleosteus Terrelli swam Sheffield Lake 350 million years ago.

Shell Cove Park

Location:
Lake Road (US 6) 200
feet west of Irving
Park Boulevard
Sheffield Lake, OH

Latitude:
N 41° 29.72'

Longitude:
W 082° 05.30'

Waterbody:
Lake Erie

**Access
Site Type:**
Recreational

Environments:
Manmade Shore

Lorain
County

The 1.5-acre Shell Cove Park is Sheffield Lake's most eastern public coastal access site. The park on U.S. Route 6 (East Lake Road) pays tribute to the region's ancient history via an expansive kiosk immediately east of the road-adjacent parking lot.

The kiosk describes the "terrible fish" now known as Dunkleosteus terrelli. The extinct, massive, joint-necked, armor-plated fish lived in the Devonian sea, which covered much of eastern North America 354-364 million years ago. Fossils of this creature were discovered here in 1867. An Ohio historical marker commemorating this is located on site.

Today, the park's upper mowed-grass area is flanked by shade trees. The grounds slope toward the center to a path leading about halfway down the 40-foot tall shale cliff to an observation deck offering scenic Lake Erie views.

Due to safety factors, this site should not be considered a fishing or shore access location. The park's shore can only be reached by climbing down concrete rubble placed lakeward of the observation deck. From the deck's viewing vantage, depending on water levels, a narrow rock beach may be present. Thousands of years of waves have smoothed the rocks and worn wave-looking patterns on their surface. Rock sizes range from boulders to small stones and are mixed with shells and shell fragments.

Additional amenities include picnic tables and grills, playground equipment and benches overlooking Lake Erie. The

Amenities and Services:

Location Map:

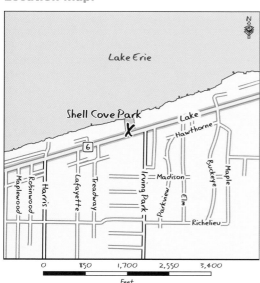

Lake Erie

Shell Cove Park

Lake

Hawthorne

6

Maplewood
Robinwood
Harris
Lafayette
Treadway
Irving Park
Madison
Parkview
Elm
Buckeye
Maple
Richelieu

| 0 | 850 | 1,700 | 2,550 | 3,400 |

Feet

Field Notes:

Date Visited: _____

Learn More:
City of Sheffield Lake
Parks and Recreation Department
(440) 949-5295
www.sheffieldlake.net

Miller Road Park

Location:
Lake (US 6) and
Miller roads
Avon Lake, OH

Latitude:
N 41° 30.16′

Longitude:
W 082° 03.58′

Waterbody:
Lake Erie

**Access
Site Type:**
Recreational

Environments:
Bluff
Sandy Beach
Manmade Shore

Lorain
County

The 17.7-acre Miller Road Park is on U.S. Route 6 (Lake Road) northeast of the Miller Road intersection on the city of Avon Lake's west side.

The park features a two-lane public boat launch accessible 24-hours a day. The launch is protected by two piers providing fishing access. The 550-foot west pier is made of limestone boulders, as is the 400-foot east pier, which is topped with a handicap accessible, paved concrete, lighted walkway. A 2002 grant from the Ohio Coastal Management Program funded, in part, the construction of a beach access ramp from the east pier down to the beach. The foot-friendly sand beach may run the length of the park's property; however, the width and length vary with water levels.

Miller Road Park is adjacent to the west of a coal-fired power plant. The nearshore waters may be warmer than surrounding Lake Erie water. Temperature differences, shore structures, and nearshore profiles can cause currents here (*see beach safety tips in the introduction*). Swimming is at one's own risk.

The back beach is lined with a twenty-foot tall shale cliff. For safety, a chain link fence runs along the top of the cliff separating the bluff face from the park's upper, partially shaded grass area. Amenities include picnic tables, grills, playgrounds, paved trails and two gazebos.

The park's west parking lot has car-trailer parking. Additional car-only lots are along the east side of park property and U.S. Route 6, which parallels the Back Roads & Beaches Bike Trail.

Lake Erie Public Access Guidebook

Field Notes:

_____

_____

_____

_____

_____

_____

Amenities and Services:

_____

_____

_____

_____

_____

_____

Location Map:

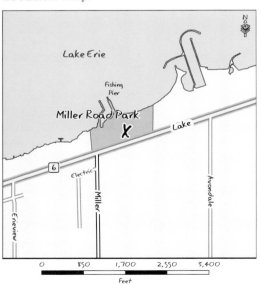

_____

_____

_____

_____

_____

_____

Date Visited: _____

Learn More:
City of Avon Lake
Parks and Recreation Department
(440) 930-4130
www.avonlake.org

Veterans Memoric

Location:
Lake Road (US 6),
west of Avon-Belden
Road (SR 83)
Avon Lake, OH

**Lat/Long
(Cemetery):**
N 41° 30.79'
W 082° 01.22'

Lat/Long (Park):
N 41° 30.80'
W 082° 01.12'

Waterbody:
Lake Erie

**Access
Site Type:**
Cultural
Scenic
Recreational

Environments:
Bluff
Sandy Beach

The 1-acre Avon Lake Cemetery and the 5.8-acre Veterans Memorial Park are on adjacent property north of U.S. Route 6 (Lake Road) at the northern terminus of State Route 83 (Avon Belden Road) in Avon Lake.

Together, the properties front 1,000 feet of shore including a 300-foot sand beach. The sand is between six groins, each extending 40 feet into Lake Erie and providing fishing access. Swimming is permitted on the beach while lifeguards are on duty (1 to 6 pm from June through Labor Day). Pets are not allowed on the beach.

A small Lake Erie tributary splits the beach between two groins at the beach's western end. The tributary also divides the park and land rented by the Avon Lake Boat Club for docking small boats and kayaks by city residents. The club's trolley system for launching boats also crosses the beach.

Veterans Park is home to a Veterans memorial, the Lake House and the Folger Home rental properties. Additional amenities include a handicap-accessible, wooden boardwalk that tops the graded grass bluff. Benches evenly spaced along the boardwalk face north allowing for scenic views. Public restrooms at Veterans Memorial Park include an outside shower.

A stone revetment fronts much of the Avon Lake Cemetery property. The cemetery has an arbor and memorial honoring veterans. Aside from benches overlooking Lake Erie, the cemetery has no amenities.

Park and Avon Lake Cemetery

Amenities and Services (Park):

Amenities and Services (Cemetery):

Location Map:

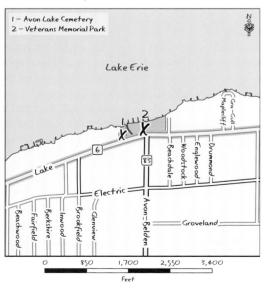

1 – Avon Lake Cemetery
2 – Veterans Memorial Park

Lake Erie

Field Notes:

Date Visited: _____

Learn More:
City of Avon Lake
Parks and Recreation Department
(440) 930-4130
www.avonlake.org

Established: June 7, 1808
2000 Population: 1,393,845
2010 Projection: 1,332,540
Land Area and Rank: 458.3 square miles, 40 of 88
County Seat: City of Cleveland
Named for: Native American word meaning "crooked river"

Miles of Coast: 30 miles
Miles of Publicly Accessible Coast: 6.1 miles
Number of Access Sites: 26

Cuyahoga County

A brief history:

Cuyahoga County was established on June 7, 1808, from a portion of Geauga County. Cuyahoga The county's name is derived from the Native American word meaning "crooked river." County's 458 square land miles were originally part of the Connecticut Western Reserve.

General Moses Cleaveland brought the first European settlers to the area in 1796. He founded the city of Cleveland that same year. With completion of the Ohio and Erie Canal and its location on Lake Erie, Cleveland prospered as a trade center and became a major industrial site. Many people from around the world came to Cleveland during the late 1800s and early 1900s looking for work in the city's industries. This is reflected today in the county's ethnic diversity; however, the county has experienced a declining population in recent years due to urban sprawl and the loss of industrial jobs.

Approximately forty-five percent of Cuyahoga County's residents earn their living by working in service industries, including in health care and communications. Other employment includes manufacturing, sales and the shipping industry. The county has three major professional sports franchises, the Cleveland Browns (football), the Cleveland Cavaliers (basketball) and the Cleveland Indians (baseball).

Among the county's more famous residents were comedian Bob Hope, 20th President of the United States James Garfield and Standard Oil founder John D. Rockefeller.

Learn More:

Cuyahoga County
www.cuyahogacounty.us

City of Bay Village
www.cityofbayvillage.com

Village of Bratenahl
www.bratenahl.org

City of Cleveland
www.city.cleveland.oh.us

City of Euclid
www.cityofeuclid.com

City of Lakewood
www.onelakewood.com

City of Rocky River
www.rrcity.com

Cleveland Metroparks
www.clemetparks.com

Euclid Chamber of Commerce
www.euclidchamber.com

Greater Cleveland Partnership
www.gcpartnership.com

Lakewood Chamber of Commerce
www.lakewoodchamber.org

Positively Cleveland
www.positivelycleveland.com

Rocky River Chamber of Commerce
www.rockyriverchamber.com

Westshore Chamber of Commerce
www.westshorechamber.org

Public Access Management:

Local	16
State	7
County	1
Metropark	1
Other	1

Lakeside Cemetery

Location:
Lake Road, west of
Pinewood Drive
Bay Village, OH

Latitude:
N 41° 29.47′

Longitude:
W 081° 56.42′

Waterbody:
Lake Erie

**Access
Site Type:**
Cultural
Scenic

Environments:
Bluff

Cuyahoga
County

The 0.7-acre Lakeside Cemetery is on U.S. Route 6 (Lake Road) just west of the Pinewood Road intersection in Bay Village. The site is Cuyahoga County's westernmost coastal public access location.

Platted in 1814, Lakeside Cemetery was the first public burying ground in Dover Township, which is now Bay Village, Westlake and the northern portion of North Olmsted. The cemetery was created after settler Reuben Osborn donated land to bury two people who drowned attempting to cross the Rocky River by boat. Additional land was later purchased to bring the site to its current size.

Internments were not recorded until 1879; however, there are more than 270 known burials. Among those interned are veterans from the Revolutionary War, the War of 1812, the Civil War, the Spanish-American War and World War I.

Direct shore access here is blocked by a black cast iron fence running the length of the cemetery.

There are no amenities at the cemetery. An access road loops the perimeter of the cemetery but there is no parking. Public parking is available approximately 1,000 feet east at Cleveland Metroparks' Huntington Reservation. An Ohio historical marker is found on site.

Field Notes:

_____

_____

_____

_____

Amenities and Services:

Location Map:

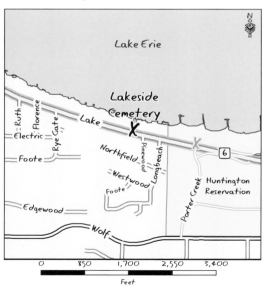

Lake Erie

Lakeside Cemetery

Lake

Ruth
Florence
Electric
Rye Gate
Foote
Northfield
Pinewood
Longbeach
6
Westwood
Foote
Huntington Reservation
Porter Creek
Edgewood
Wolf

0   850   1,700   2,550   3,400

Feet

N

Cuyahoga County

Date Visited: _____

Learn More:
City of Bay Village
440-871-2200
www.cityofbayvillage.com

Huntington Reser

Location:
Lake Road (US 6) and
Porter Creek Drive
28728 Wolf Road
Bay Village, OH

Latitude:
N 41° 29.42'

Longitude:
W 081° 56.15'

Waterbody:
Lake Erie

**Access
Site Type:**
Recreational

Environments:
Bluff
Sandy Beach

The 102-acre Cleveland Metroparks Huntington Reservation straddles U.S. Route 6 (Lake Road) with the coastal access parking lot at the north terminus of Porter Creek Drive.

Stretching 0.4 miles, Huntington's foot-friendly sand beach is one of Cuyahoga County's most popular. The beach width varies between the five groins which extend up to 400 feet into Lake Erie. These structures help stabilize the shore and provide year-round fishing access.

The NOWcast system for predicting water quality, (*see water quality monitoring in the introduction*) was pioneered at Huntington Beach. The computer model's accuracy has spurred researchers to start establishing NOWcast systems at five additional Ohio Lake Erie swimming beaches.

The beach is accessible via sets of stairs that traverse the steep bluff. At the reservation's eastern end an Americans with Disabilities Act (ADA) compliant parking lot and beach-access walkway built in 2006 was funded, in part, by an Ohio Coastal Management Program grant.

Picnic tables and grills are scattered throughout the upper park area which includes many amenities such as concessions and restrooms. A bluff-side trail connects to the all-purpose, 1-mile Porter Creek Trail which connects to the city of Bay Village's bike trail. The reservation is home to three Cleveland Metroparks affiliates: Lake Erie Nature and Science Center, Huntington Playhouse and BayArts.

The Huntington Water Tower, which is listed on the National Register of Historic Places, was used to pump water to irrigate vineyards.

vation

Amenities and Services:

Location Map:

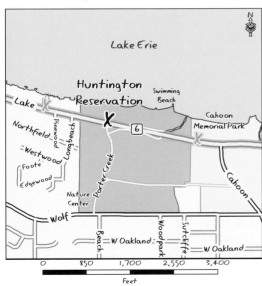

Lake Erie

Huntington Reservation

Swimming Beach

Cahoon Memorial Park

Lake

Northfield

Pinewood

Longbeach

Westwood

Foote

Edgewood

6

Porter Creek

Cahoon

Nature Center

Wolf

Beach

W Oakland

Woodpark

Sutcliffe

W Oakland

0   850   1,700   2,550   3,400

Feet

Cuyahoga County

Date Visited: _____

Learn More:
Cleveland Metroparks
(216) 635-3200
www.clemetparks.com

Cahoon Memorial

Occupying 116 acres of partially shaded land east of the Huntington Reservation, west of Dover Center Road and north of Wolf Road, the city of Bay Village's Cahoon Memorial Park has nearly 2,300 feet of coastal access.

The portion of Cahoon Memorial Park north of U.S. Route 6 (Lake Road) is divided by the Cahoon Creek into two access points. For safety purposes (at both access areas), a chain-link fence runs along the top of the bluff which is experiencing varying degrees of erosion. Benches and picnic tables allow for scenic Lake Erie views.

The parking lot for the 13.7-acre west ("Cahoon") access is north of Lake Road about 450 feet west the Cahoon Road intersection. A half-mile paved asphalt exercise trail circles this parcel. No bicycles or skateboards are allowed on the trail.

Cahoon Memorial Park's east ("Dover") access is at the north terminus of Bryson Lane. The 6.7-acre parcel is home to the Bay Boat Club's two-lane, small-boat launch. Membership to the public club is open to any Bay Village boat-owning resident.

Most of Cahoon Park's amenities are located in the non-coastal section south of Lake Road. The park is open 5 am to 11 pm daily, but closed Sundays.

Park

Location Map:

Lake Erie

Cahoon Memorial Park

West

East

6

Boat Club

Huntington Reservation

Museum

Cahoon

Bryson

Lake

Bruce

Swimming Pool

Russell

Dover Center

Wolf

Woodpark

Sutcliffe

W Oakland

Normandy

0 | 850 | 1,700 | 2,550 | 3,400

Feet

Cuyahoga County

Field Notes:

Date Visited: _____

Learn More:
City of Bay Village
Recreation Department
(440) 871-6755
www.cityofbayvillage.com

Columbia Park

Location:
Lake (US 6) and Columbia (SR 252)
Bay Village, OH

Latitude:
N 41° 29.14'

Longitude:
W 081° 54.10'

Waterbody:
Lake Erie

Access Site Type:
Scenic

Environments:
Bluff
Riparian/River
Sandy Beach

Cuyahoga County

The melody of water cascading from a 40-foot tall shale bluff, pooling at the bottom, and then flowing into Lake Erie is a predominant feature of the city of Bay Village's 1.6-acre Columbia Park.

This quaint access site is north of U.S. Route 6 (Lake Road) at the northwest corner of the Columbia Road (State Route 252) intersection. Parking is available on the south side of Lake Road in a small lot west of Columbia Road.

From the sidewalk, a paved walkway leads through the center of a mowed-grass green space to a steep bluff face topped by a concrete platform. The platform is surrounded by a green chain-link safety fence. To the west, an observation deck overlooks a small creek. At the base of the bluff (and waterfall), this Lake Erie tributary crosses a 15-foot wide beach – a mixture of glacial till, shale stones, sand and shell fragments.

The beach is accessible by traversing 67 concrete steps with another observation platform four feet above the beach near the base of the steps. Signage at the park notes that the beach is not guarded and the water may be contaminated after rain events. A bike rack and trash cans are in the upper park area. Columbia Park closes at dusk.

Amenities and Services:

Location Map:

Lake Erie

Columbia
Park

6

252

Canterbury
Kenilworth
Parkside
Huntmere
Oakmoor
Lake Forest
Osborn
Juneway
Columbia
Bayfair
Wolf
Lakeview
Sunset
Lake
Electric
Forestview

0   850   1,700   2,550   3,400

Feet

Field Notes:

_____
_____
_____
_____
_____
_____
_____
_____
_____
_____
_____
_____
_____
_____
_____
_____
_____
_____
_____

Date Visited: _____

Learn More:
City of Bay Village
Recreation Department
(440) 871-6755
www.cityofbayvillage.com

Bradstreet's Lan

Location:
Lake Road (US 6),
west of Avalon Ave
Rocky River, OH

Latitude:
N 41° 28.93'

Longitude:
W 081° 52.07'

Waterbody:
Lake Erie

**Access
Site Type:**
Recreational

Environments:
Riparian/River
Sandy Beach

Cuyahoga
County

The 6-acre Bradstreet's Landing is north of U.S. Route 6 (Lake Road) just east of the East Pond Drive intersection in the city of Rocky River.

The landing's predominate feature is a 600-foot long, 20-foot wide fishing pier rising more than 20 feet above the surface of Lake Erie. The handicap accessible, paved concrete fishing pier is surrounded by chain link fence and safety rails. Bicycles are prohibited on the pier. A bike rack is located at the foot of the pier on the east side.

Green space in the partially-shaded upper area of the Bradstreet's Landing includes amenities including picnic areas, a picnic deck, concession building/bait store and paved trails. This site has a 125-foot sand beach west of the pier. A small groin marks the beach area's western extent. The east side of the park is accessible by crossing a wooden footbridge over a small Lake Erie tributary. A wooded area lines the back of this 300-foot long sand beach.

Per city regulation, swimming and wading are not allowed at Bradstreet's Landing; however, launching of windsurfers and sailboats is permitted from the east beach. Posted warnings remind water-users to stay clear of fishing lines extending from the pier. Launching of power boats, jet skis and inflatable watercraft is prohibited.

Park hours are sunrise to sunset.

ding

Amenities and Services:

Location Map:

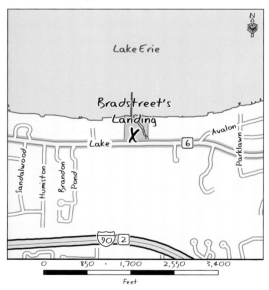

Lake Erie

Bradstreet's
Landing

Lake   6   Avalon

Sandalwood Humiston Brandon Pond Parklawn

90 2

0   850   1,700   2,550   3,400
Feet

Field Notes:

_____
_____
_____
_____
_____
_____
_____
_____
_____
_____
_____
_____
_____
_____
_____
_____
_____
_____
_____

Date Visited: _____

Learn More:
City of Rocky River
Parks and Recreation
(440) 356-5657
www.rrcity.com

Rocky River Park

Location:
Beach Cliff Boulevard
and Kensington Oval
20250 Beach
Cliff Boulevard
Rocky River, OH

Latitude:
N 41° 29.22'

Longitude:
W 081° 50.76'

Waterbody:
Lake Erie

**Access
Site Type:**
Recreational

Environments:
Bluff
Sandy Beach
Manmade Shore

Cuyahoga
County

The 6-acre Rocky River Park is located north of Beach Cliff Boulevard with parking access off Parkside Drive. In 2006, the park underwent $100,000 in improvements including erosion control measures, thus creating a terrace and amphitheater effect.

Along the park's east side, a handicap accessible paved walkway is separated by a green chain-link safety fence from a low, steep, vegetated bluff at the back of the beach. The walkway leads to a 180-foot pier marking the park's eastern edge. The park has a 475-foot sand beach fronted by a breakwater; however, swimming, wading, fishing, boat launching and climbing on the erosion control structure are prohibited per city regulation.

The graded, grass-covered bluff on the park's west side is separated from the beach by a concrete block seawall.

Park amenities include picnic facilities, playground equipment and benches offering Lake Erie views. The park is open from 6 am to sunset.

During summer months, Rocky River Park is home to the Sunset Concert Series.

Field Notes:

_____

_____

_____

_____

_____

_____

_____

_____

Amenities and Services:

Location Map:

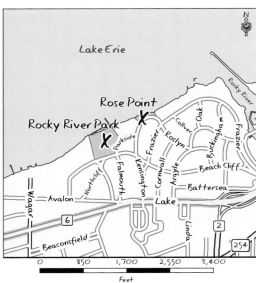

Learn More:
City of Rocky River
Parks and Recreation
(440) 356-5657
www.rrcity.com

Date Visited: _____

Cuyahoga County

Rose Point

The 0.8-acre Rose Point is a scenic overlook in Rocky River along the northern portion of Kensington Oval just west of Frazier Drive. Along the coast, the Rose Point is just 530 feet east of Rocky River Park; by road Rose Point is approximately 1,200 feet east.

The top of the vegetated bluff is marked by a wooden split-rail fence which runs the point's 325-foot length. The width of this scenic overlook ranges from just 6 feet in the center to 70 feet and 60 feet on the respective west and east ends. This mowed-grass green space has park benches overlooking Lake Erie. A few small deciduous trees are planted near the benches.

The steep bluff is covered with vegetative grasses and a few small shrubs. Attempting to traverse the bluff would be difficult. The base of the bluff is marked by a concrete block revetment erosion control structure. Generally, a beach is not present.

Field Notes:

_____
_____
_____
_____
_____
_____
_____
_____
_____
_____
_____
_____
_____
_____
_____
_____
_____
_____
_____

Date Visited: _____

Amenities and Services:

Location Map:

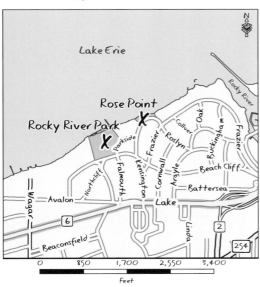

Cuyahoga County

Learn More:
City of Rocky River
(440) 331-0600
www.rrcity.com

City of Lakewood

Location (Webb):
End of Webb Road, north
of Edgewater Drive
Lakewood, OH

Lat/Long (Webb):
N 41° 29.61'
W 081° 49.21'

Location (Summit):
End of Summit Avenue,
north of Edgewater Drive
Lakewood, OH

Lat/Long (Summit):
N 41° 29.73'
W 081° 48.41'

Location (Cliff):
Cliff Drive, west of
Wilbert Road; also
fenced area between
Wilbert Road and
Nicholson Avenue
Lakewood, OH

Lat/Long (Cliff):
N 41° 29.74'
W 081° 47.10'

In Lakewood, three publicly accessible road rights-of-way provide scenic Lake Erie views. Starting on the west, they are Webb Road and Summit Avenue both of which intersect with Clifton Boulevard (U.S. routes 6 and 20 and State Route 2, respectively). The third, Cliff Drive, is accessible from Nicholson Avenue which also intersects Clifton Boulevard.

Webb Road's pavement ends 160 feet from the top of the bluff. Within the road right-of-way, a 0.21-acre lighted, mowed-grass green space continues lakeward. A bench at the north end overlooks Lake Erie. Direct lake access is prevented by a chain-link fence.

A mile east is the 0.12-acre Summit Avenue scenic overlook. Similar to Webb Road, Summit Avenue's pavement ends approximately 90 feet from the bluff. The right-of-way continues as a mowed green space. Two park benches overlook Lake Erie. A chain-link fence prohibits access to the water.

Driving 1.6 miles east, Cliff Drive parallels the Lake Erie shore atop a steep bluff. The drive dead-ends just west of Wilbert Road and extends east to Nicholson Avenue. The north side of Cliff Drive is open to the lake and lined with a chain-link fence. Sporadic deciduous trees in danger of succumbing to erosion line the top of the bluff. West of Cliff Drive's western terminus, the road right-of way is maintained by the city of Lakewood as a small mowed-grass green space. Looking east, this area allows for views of downtown Cleveland. There are no amenities on site.

Scenic Accesses

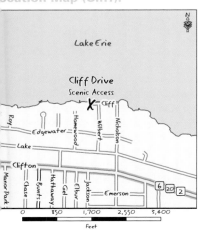

Waterbody (All):
Lake Erie

**Access
Site Type (All):**
Scenic
Right-of-Way

Environments (All):
Bluff

**Amenities and
Services (Webb):**

**Amenities and
Services (Summit):**

**Amenities and
Services (Cliff):**
None

Learn More:
City of Lakewood
Department of Public Works
Division of Parks and Public Property
(216) 529-6815
www.onelakewood.com

Cuyahoga County

Lakewood Park

Location:
Lake Avenue, at
Belle Avenue
14532 Lake Avenue
Lakewood, OH

Latitude:
N 41° 29.71'

Longitude:
W 081° 47.81'

Waterbody:
Lake Erie

**Access
Site Type:**
Recreational

Environments:
Bluff
Manmade Shore

Cuyahoga
County

The 40.5-acre Lakewood Park is on Lake Avenue at Belle Avenue in the city of Lakewood. Additional access points and parking are available on the park's west side, and also on the park's east side from the intersection of Parkside and Edgewater drives.

Lakewood Park provides one-third mile of coastal access; however, the 14 acres that comprise the majority of the shore is fill material that was placed in Lake Erie from 1935 to 1956. A revetment helps prevent erosion along the park's entire shore. Along the top of the revetment on the park's north and west sides is Lakefront Promenade, which was completed in 2006. Construction of this Americans with Disabilities Act (ADA) compliant, brick paver walkway was paid for in part with a 2003 grant from the Ohio Coastal Management Program. The path extends from the top of the bluff at the northeast corner of the park's property down to the lower promenade. The promenade provides scenic views of downtown Cleveland aided by stationary binoculars placed along the path.

Lakewood Park does not have a beach; however, one of the city's two public outdoor swimming pools is located here. Additional amenities at the partially shaded Lakewood Park include picnic shelters and tables, grills, playground equipment, a bandstand, a paved trail network, sand volleyball courts, baseball fields and a skate park. The Women's Club, Kiwanis Pavilion and the Oldest Stone House Museum are also on site.

LAKEWOOD PARK

Amenities and Services:

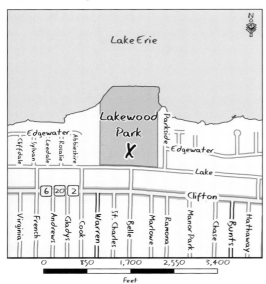

Location Map:

Lake Erie

Lakewood
Park
X

Edgewater

Edgewater

Parkside

Lake

Clifton

6 20 2

Cliffdale
Sylvan
Leedale
Rosalie
Abbieshire

Virginia
French
Andrews
Gladys
Cook
Warren
St. Charles
Belle
Marlowe
Ramona
Manor Park
Chase
Bunts
Hathaway

0   850   1,700   2,550   3,400
Feet

Cuyahoga
County

Field Notes:

_____

_____

_____

_____

_____

_____

_____

_____

_____

_____

_____

_____

_____

_____

_____

_____

_____

_____

Date Visited: _____

Learn More:
City of Lakewood
Department of Public Works
Division of Parks and Public Property
(216) 529-6815
www.onelakewood.com

Cleveland Lakefront State Park
Edgewater Park

Location:

Upper section entrance:
Just north of West Blvd
and Edgewater Dr.
Cleveland, OH

Lower section entrance:
Freeway exit off
Cleveland Memorial
Shoreway

Boat ramp entrance:
Whiskey Island Drive,
east of Cleveland
Memorial Shoreway
freeway exit

Lat/Long (park):
N 41° 29.37'
W 081° 44.29'

Lat/Long (ramp):
N 41° 29.65'
W 081° 43.65'

Cuyahoga County

Waterbody:
Lake Erie

**Access
Site Type:**
Recreational
Impervious/Pier

Environments:
Bluff
Sandy Beach
Manmade Shore

The 134.5-acre Edgewater Park is the westernmost park in the Cleveland Lakefront State Park system. Located north of Cleveland Memorial Shoreway (U.S. routes 6 and 20 and State Route 2), this site features upper and lower sections connected by the paved Cleveland Lakefront Bikeway and a fitness course.

Edgewater's upper, western section is on Cliff Drive and accessible from West Boulevard. The expansive, partially-shaded green space is primarily a picnic grounds with trails, and has a 0.46-mile bluff overlooking Lake Erie. This upper section is separated from the lower by a large sloping hill, popularly used for sledding during winter.

Edgewater's lower, eastern section is accessible via an exit ramp off the Shoreway. The lower park includes a half-mile sand beach; the easternmost 900 feet of which are groomed, and 400-feet-wide. Two picnic shelters and a bathhouse are located between the beach and an expansive parking lot.

North of the parking lot, an open mowed grass field is used for, among other activities, flying kites. A second parking lot and a concession stand are closer to the shore. This area of Edgewater is protected from erosion by a 2,360-foot revetment/seawall which provides fishing access as does a 200-foot fishing pier.

The disjoined eight-lane Edgewater Boat Ramp is located off Ed Hauser Way just east of Edgewater Marina. The boat launch has an L-shaped tie-up dock and two parking lots within walking distance. Fishing is permitted in this area.

and Boat Ramp

Amenities and Services (park):

Amenities and Services (ramp):

Location Map:

N

Lake Erie

Edgewater
Boat Ramp

Fishing
Pier

Yacht Club
(private)

Edgewater Park

East
Entrance

Swimming
Beach

Cliff

Edgewater

West
Entrance

West

Clifton

Baltic

Desmond

Lake

W. 85th

W. 76th

W. 75th

W. 69th

W. 65th

Detroit

Franklin

6 20 2

0   1,250   2,500   3,750   5,000

Feet

Field Notes:

Date Visited: _____

Learn More:
ODNR Division of Parks and Recreation
ohiodnr.com/parks
ohiodnr.com/tabid/721/default.aspx

Cuyahoga
County

Wendy Park

Location:
Eastern terminus of
Ed Hauser Way
Cleveland, OH

Latitude:
N 41° 29.92'

Longitude:
W 081° 42.88'

Waterbody:
Lake Erie
Cuyahoga River

**Access
Site Type:**
Recreational

Environments:
Riparian/River
Sandy Beach
Manmade Shore

The 25.4-acre Wendy Park, at the eastern terminus Ed Hauser Way (formerly Whiskey Island Drive), provides access to both Lake Erie and the Cuyahoga River. The park's access road is reached via the Edgewater Park freeway ramp off Cleveland Memorial Shoreway (U.S. routes 6 and 20 and State Route 2).

Traveling the length of Ed Hauser Way provides a glimpse of Cleveland's industrial heritage as it parallels networks of railroad tracks and passes piles of iron pellets and salt, a marina and a water treatment plant.

Whiskey Island was named after a distillery that was built on the land in the 1830s. The "island" is actually now a peninsula, but when the Cuyahoga River mouth was relocated to its current location in 1827 to straighten the shipping channel, the land was surrounded by water. The old river mouth was filled in the 1920s, and the "island" was no more. In 2004, Cuyahoga County purchased the land that includes the park and Whiskey Island Marina.

The county's purchase of Wendy Park was spurred by the Friends of Whiskey Island, led by the late, citizen-activist Ed Hauser for whom the access road was dedicated in 2009. The park features sand volleyball courts, a picnic area, trails and fishing access. The park's Cuyahoga River access includes a 1,440-foot paved pier connecting to the historic Coast Guard station. Wendy Park also affords scenic views of downtown Cleveland.

Amenities and Services:

Location Map:

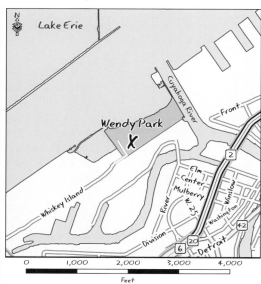

Date Visited: _____

Learn More:
Wendy Park Foundation
(216) 904-9456
www.wendyparkfoundation.org

North Coast Ha

Location:
East 9th Street and
Erieside Avenue
Cleveland, OH

Latitude:
N 41° 30.47′

Longitude:
W 081° 41.76′

Waterbody:
Lake Erie

**Access
Site Type:**
Cultural

Environments:
Manmade Shore

The North Coast Harbor, East Ninth Street Pier and Voinov-ich Bicentennial Park areas are east and north of Erieside Avenue, three-quarters of a mile east of the Cuyahoga River mouth in downtown Cleveland. The majority of the park's land is fill material artificially placed in Lake Erie. The public walkway surrounding these areas includes more than a mile of manmade shore.

The 3.3-acre North Coast Harbor includes public green space, a paved concrete pier and walkway and two popular attractions - the Great Lakes Science Center including the Steamship *William G. Mather* and the Rock and Roll Hall of Fame and Museum. Entering these attractions requires admission fees.

A skate park and an Ohio Historical Marker honoring the history of Rock-n-Roll are on site. The Cleveland Lakefront Bikeway follows the Lake Erie shore through the harbor grounds.

This location affords picturesque views of the downtown Cleveland skyline.

...or

Amenities and Services:

Location Map:

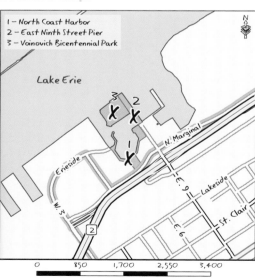

1 – North Coast Harbor
2 – East Ninth Street Pier
3 – Voinovich Bicentennial Park

Lake Erie

N. Marginal
Erieside
E. 9
Lakeside
W 3
E. 6
St. Clair

0   850   1,700   2,550   3,400

Feet

Cuyahoga County

Field Notes:

Date Visited: _____

Learn More:
City of Cleveland
Department of Parks, Recreation &
Properties
(216) 664-2485
www.city.cleveland.oh.us

East Ninth Street

Location:
End of East 9th Street
Cleveland, OH

Latitude:
N 41° 30.61'

Longitude:
W 081° 41.74'

Waterbody:
Lake Erie

**Access
Site Type:**
Impervious
Pier

Environments:
Manmade Shore

Cuyahoga
County

The North Coast Harbor, East Ninth Street Pier and Voi-novich Bicentennial Park areas are east and north of Erie-side Avenue, three-quarter mile east of the Cuyahoga River mouth in downtown Cleveland.

The public walkway surrounding these areas includes a more than a mile of manmade shore.

The L-shaped East Ninth Street Pier is adjacent to the east of North Coast Harbor at the northern terminus of East Ninth Street. Fishing and parking are permitted in desig-nated areas on the handicap-accessible paved pier. The pier is also the docking/boarding site for the Goodtime III scenic boat charter.

This location affords picturesque views of the downtown skyline.

Pier

Amenities and Services:

Location Map:

1 – North Coast Harbor
2 – East Ninth Street Pier
3 – Voinovich Bicentennial Park

N

Lake Erie

3
2

N. Marginal

Erieside

E. 9
Lakeside

W. W

2

E. 6
St. Clair

0   850   1,700   2,550   3,400
Feet

Cuyahoga County

Field Notes:

_____
_____
_____
_____
_____
_____
_____
_____
_____
_____
_____
_____
_____
_____
_____
_____
_____
_____
_____

Date Visited: _____

Learn More:
City of Cleveland
Department of Parks, Recreation &
Properties
(216) 664-2485
www.city.cleveland.oh.us

Voinovich Bicent

Location:
End of East
9th Street Pier
Cleveland, OH

Latitude:
N 41° 30.62'

Longitude:
W 081° 41.83'

Waterbody:
Lake Erie

**Access
Site Type:**
Scenic

Environments:
Manmade Shore

Cuyahoga
County

The North Coast Harbor, East Ninth Street Pier and Voinovich Bicentennial Park areas are east and north of Erieside Avenue, three-quarter mile east of the Cuyahoga River mouth in downtown Cleveland. The majority of the park's land is fill material artificially placed in Lake Erie. The public walkway surrounding these areas includes a more than a mile of manmade shore.

The 4.5-acre Voinovich Bicentennial Park is at the north end of the East Ninth Street Pier, along the pier's west side. Voinovich Park's center is a large, artistically-terraced green space which is surrounded by impervious surface areas. The park's southwest corner has a concrete stage. Fishing is permitted in designated areas.

Voinovich Bicentennial Park hosts a variety of festivals and events during summer months, some of which require admission fees. This location also affords picturesque views of the downtown Cleveland skyline.

nial Park

Amenities and Services:

Location Map:

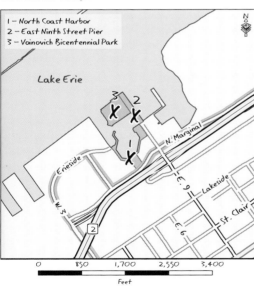

1 – North Coast Harbor
2 – East Ninth Street Pier
3 – Voinovich Bicentennial Park

Lake Erie

0   850   1,700   2,550   3,400
Feet

Cuyahoga County

Date Visited: _____

Learn More:
City of Cleveland
Department of Parks, Recreation &
Properties
(216) 664-2485
www.city.cleveland.oh.us

Cleveland Lakefront State Park
East 55th Street

Location:
North Marginal Road
and East 55th Stree
Cleveland, OH

Latitude:
N 41° 32.05'

Longitude:
W 081° 38.87'

Waterbody:
Lake Erie

**Access
Site Type:**
Recreational

Environments:
Manmade Shore

Cuyahoga
County

The 20.2-acre East 55th Street Marina is one of six sites in the Cleveland Lakefront State Park system. The marina is on North Marginal Road near the north end of East 55th Street, about 2.25 miles east of Burke Lakefront Airport's entrance.

Inside a sizable manmade harbor, the marina has 335 seasonal rental docks with water and electric hookups. A marina concession facility is in the southeast corner of the park. Expansive connected parking areas line the property's east and south sides. Mowed grass areas surround each lot. Restroom facilities, picnic areas and a playground are found in these open spaces.

Fishing is allowed throughout the park which touches the open waters of Lake Erie and the protected marina area. The north side of East 55th Street Marina is protected by a 0.42-mile bulkhead pier. The majority of the north pier has an unpaved dirt trail running its length; deciduous trees also grow sporadically atop. The eastern portion of the pier along with the bulkhead protecting the park's east side is un-shaded, handicap-accessible paved concrete. Down a step, the capped-concrete bulkhead continues nearly 800 feet parallel to the north of the Cleveland Memorial Shoreway (State Route 2 and U.S. Route 90).

The Cleveland Lakefront Bikeway passes through the south of the park, directly connecting it to Gordon Park, a coastal access site to the east.

Marina

Amenities and Services:

Location Map:

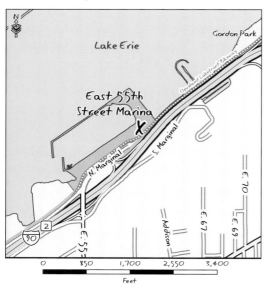

Lake Erie

Gordon Park

Cleveland Lakefront Parkway

East 55th
Street Marina

N. Marginal

S. Marginal

Addison

E. 67

E. 69

E. 70

E. 55

2

90

| 0 | 850 | 1,700 | 2,550 | 3,400 |

Feet

Cuyahoga
County

Field Notes:

_____

_____

_____

_____

_____

_____

_____

_____

_____

_____

_____

_____

_____

_____

_____

_____

_____

Date Visited: _____

Learn More:
ODNR Division of Parks and Recreation
ohiodnr.com/parks
ohiodnr.com/tabid/721/default.aspx

Cleveland Lakefront State Park
Gordon Park

Location:
Lake Shore Boulevard
and Dr. Martin Luther
King Jr. Drive
8701 Lake Shore
Boulevard, NE
Cleveland, OH

Latitude:
N 41° 32.52'

Longitude:
W 081° 37.74'

Waterbody:
Lake Erie

**Access
Site Type:**
Recreational

Environments:
Manmade Shore

Cuyahoga
County

The 51.5-acre Gordon Park houses the headquarters of the six-site Cleveland Lakefront State Park system. Gordon Park has multiple access points, with the main entrance and park office off Lake Shore Boulevard.

The west end of Lake Shore Boulevard connects to Martin Luther King, Jr. Drive; the drive also connects to the east end of North Marginal Road. Gordon Park's six-lane boat launch and car-trailer parking lot are accessed from the North Marginal Road entrance. Vehicle traffic is not permitted to travel from the east section of North Marginal Road to the portion of the road where East 55th Street Marina is located. However, the paved Cleveland Lakefront Bikeway directly connects the two parks via a footbridge.

Gordon Park is a mix of open and partially shaded green space and picnic areas. Fishing access is provided along the park's 1.3 miles of armored coast, including the lengths of various piers and revetments that comprise the park's entirely manmade shore and surround the park's marina. A parking lot west of the marina can be accessed from East 72nd Street.

The Cleveland Electric & Illuminating Company (operated by First Energy Corp.) has warm water discharge adjacent to the east of Gordon Park. The power plant's warm water discharge into Lake Erie attracts fish and birds, especially during winter months when the rest of the lake may be covered by ice.

Amenities and Services:

Location Map:

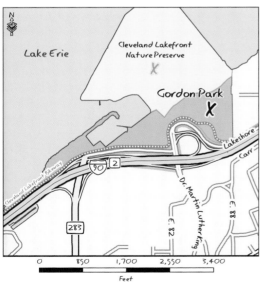

Lake Erie

Cleveland Lakefront
Nature Preserve
X

Gordon Park
X

Lakeshore

Carr

Cleveland Lakefront Parkway

90 2

283

Dr. Martin Luther King

E. 82

E. 88

0   850   1,700   2,550   3,400

Feet

Cuyahoga
County

Date Visited: _____

Learn More:
ODNR Division of Parks and Recreation
ohiodnr.com/parks
ohiodnr.com/tabid/721/default.aspx

Cleveland Lakefro

Location:
Lake Shore Boulevard
and Dr. Martin Luther
King Jr. Drive
8601 Lakeshore
Boulevard, NE
(state park address)
Cleveland, OH

Latitude:
N 41° 32.69'

Longitude:
W 081° 37.97'

Waterbody:
Lake Erie

**Access
Site Type:**
Natural

Environments:
Manmade Shore

The 88-acre Cleveland Lakefront Nature Preserve, commonly known as Dike 14, provides 1.2 miles of manmade shore access. It is adjacent to Gordon Park and accessed from the northern terminus of Martin Luther King, Jr. Drive.

The wild, green oasis in downtown Cleveland is 4.7 miles east of the mouth of the Cuyahoga River – a river to which the preserve traces its existence. Dike 14 was created in 1976 and used until 1999 to hold the spoils from dredging Cleveland's harbor and the river.

The mud and silt has metamorphosed into a haven for plants, animals and birds. Plants have colonized the preserve creating fields, wet meadows, shrub communities and stands of maturing trees. Wildlife including deer, fox, raccoons and coyotes, along with dozens of species of butterflies, reptiles, amphibians and a host of other organisms call the preserve home.

The preserve is an important staging area for migrating birds with more than 290 different species recorded. In 2004, it was recognized as an Important Bird Area by the National Audubon Society. The same year, a grant from the Ohio Coastal Management Program funded, in part, a feasibility study for safe public access to the preserve. Future site plans include creating additional trails, scenic overlooks and educational signage that balances nature and the public's passive use of the site.

t Nature Preserve

Amenities and Services (Villa):

Location Map:

Lake Erie

Cleveland Lakefront
Nature Preserve
X

Gordon
Park
X

Lakeshore

Dr. Martin Luther King

Carr

90 2

0   850   1,700   2,550   3,400
Feet

Field Notes:

_____

_____

_____

_____

_____

_____

_____

_____

_____

_____

_____

_____

_____

_____

Date Visited: _____

Learn More:
Earth Day Coalition
(216) 281-6468
www.earthdaycoalition.org
or
Cleveland Lakefront Nature Preserve
www.dike14.org

Cleveland Lakefront State Park
Euclid Beach Area

Location:
Lake Shore Boulevard
(SR 283), east of
East 156th Street
Cleveland, OH

Latitude:
N 41° 34.99'

Longitude:
W 081° 34.16'

Waterbody:
Lake Erie

**Access
Site Type:**
Recreational

Environments:
Bluff
Sandy Beach

Cuyahoga
County

The 18.9-acre Euclid Beach Area is one of six sites in the Cleveland Lakefront State Park system. The park's access road is north off State Route 283 (Lake Shore Boulevard) one-third mile east of the East 156th Street intersection.

The Euclid Beach Area was added to the Cleveland Lakefront State Park system in 1982, but its recreational history dates back to 1895 when the very popular Euclid Beach Amusement Park opened on site. The amusement park closed in 1969 and its roller coasters and rides were either relocated or razed.

Today, in the state park and surrounding privately held land, vestiges of several attractions are visible. These include the former shuffleboard area, remnants of the beach-side fountain, and concrete footers from the *Flying Turns* roller coaster's loading station and track. The only remaining fully intact structure is the former amusement park's entrance arch, a Cleveland Historic Landmark, which is over East 159th Street north of Lake Shore Boulevard.

Euclid Beach features a foot-friendly sand swimming beach. Shore access connects directly to the swimming beach at the adjacent Villa Angela Area, creating nearly a half-mile of publicly accessible coast. Additional amenities at Euclid Beach include picnic shelters, a rentable pavilion, bathhouse, playground equipment, trails and a concession stand. Fishing is permitted. The Cleveland Lakefront Bikeway is routed through Euclid Beach.

Amenities and Services:

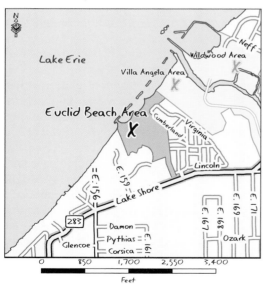

Location Map:

Lake Erie

Wildwood Area

Neff

Villa Angela Area

Euclid Beach Area

Cumberland

Virginia

Lincoln

E. 156

E. 159

Lake Shore

283

Damon

Pythias

Corsica

E. 161

Glencoe

E. 167

E. 168

E. 169

E. 171

Ozark

0   850   1,700   2,550   3,400

Feet

Field Notes:

Date Visited: _____

Learn More:
ODNR Division of Parks and Recreation
ohiodnr.com/parks
ohiodnr.com/tabid/721/default.aspx

Villa Angela and

Location:
Lake Shore Boulevard
(SR 283) at East
174th Street
Cleveland, OH

Lat/Long (Villa):
N 41° 35.14'
W 081° 33.98'

**Lat/Long
(Wildwood):**
N 41° 35.19'
W 081° 33.71'

Waterbody:
Lake Erie
Euclid Creek

**Access
Site Type:**
Recreational

Environments:
Bluff
Riparian/River
Sandy Beach
Manmade Shore

Cuyahoga
County

The 69.6 acres that comprise the adjacent Villa Angela and Wildwood areas are the two easternmost portions of the six-site Cleveland Lakefront State Park system. Park Road, at the northern terminus of East 174th Street at the State Route 283 (Lake Shore Boulevard) intersection, provides access to a main parking lot that serves both areas. Euclid Creek, a small Lake Erie tributary, divides the parks.

Villa Angela is adjacent to the north of Cleveland Public Library's Memorial-Nottingham Branch. Villa Angela features a scenic boardwalk leading out to a fishing pier, small areas of open green space and a heavily shaded area. Villa Angela's swimming beach is seamlessly connected to Euclid Beach's beach creating nearly a half-mile of publicly accessible shore. Breakwaters protect foot-friendly sand on the beach, which has an average width of 120 feet.

The Wildwood Area features a picnic area, concessions, playground equipment, a four-lane boat launch, gasoline pumps, fishing and SCUBA diving charters, a bait shop and a pocket beach inside the marina's protected area. The marina has 12 seasonal and four overnight docks and is surrounded by concrete block fishing piers. The piers, along with various other structures and reaches of shore, provide more than two-thirds mile of waterline.

The handicap-accessible, paved Cleveland Lakefront Bikeway connects the Euclid Beach, Villa Angela and Wildwood state park areas. Other trails meander through the parks.

Wildwood areas

Amenities and Services (Villa):

Amenities and Services (Wildwood):

Location Map:

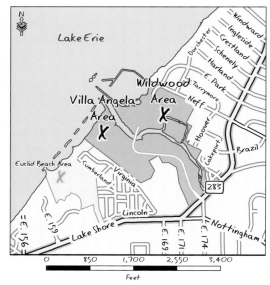

Field Notes:

_____
_____
_____
_____
_____
_____
_____
_____
_____
_____
_____
_____
_____
_____
_____
_____

Date Visited: _____

Learn More:
ODNR Division of Parks and Recreation
ohiodnr.com/parks
ohiodnr.com/tabid/721/default.aspx

Cuyahoga County

Euclid Park

The 3.5-acre Euclid Park is accessed off Bliss Lane at the north terminus of East 222nd Street/Babbitt Road intersection with State Route 283 (Lake Shore Boulevard) on the city of Euclid's east side. Bliss Lane ends in the parking lot for the on-site Euclid Community Center.

The parking lot's east and west sides are connected by a compacted gravel trail that loops the perimeter of the park in a 0.2-mile U-shape. The center of Euclid Park is mowed-grass green space. Deciduous trees line the park's eastern boundary and are sporadically planted in the park's open area. North of the trail, park benches overlooking Lake Erie line the top of a partially-mowed grass, partially-vegetated gentle slope leading down to a stone revetment at the back of the beach.

The beach area is split by a water outlet that is flanked on both sides by approximately 200-foot limestone block jetties. On the 50-foot wide, 230-foot long western beach area, the foot-friendly sand is mixed with small rocks and shell fragments near the water's edge and small pieces of driftwood at the back of the beach. The east beach is 65 feet long and averages less than 20 feet wide.

Per city regulation, swimming and other forms of water contact are not permitted at Euclid's public beaches. A small gazebo is also on site.

Field Notes:

_____

_____

_____

_____

_____

_____

_____

_____

_____

_____

_____

_____

_____

_____

_____

_____

_____

_____

Amenities and Services:

       P

Location Map:

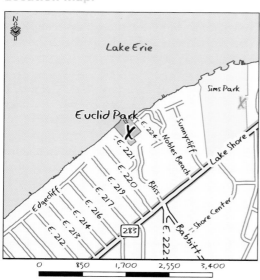

Lake Erie

Sims Park

Euclid Park

Sunnycliff
Nobles Beach
Lake Shore
E. 224
E. 221
E. 220
E. 219
E. 217
E. 216
Bliss
Edgecliff
E. 214
E. 213
E. 212
283
Rabbitt
Shore Center
E. 222

0   850   1,700   2,550   3,400

Feet

Date Visited: _____

Learn More:
City of Euclid
(216) 289-2700
www.cityofeuclid.com

Sims Park

Location:
Lake Shore Boulevard
(SR 283) at
East 232nd Street
Euclid, OH

Latitude:
N 41° 36.91'

Longitude:
W 081° 31.28'

Waterbody:
Lake Erie

**Access
Site Type:**
Recreational

Environments:
Bluff
Sandy Beach

Cuyahoga County

The 33.2-acre Sims Park is north of State Route 283 (Lake Shore Boulevard) with the park's main access road just west of East 232nd Street in Euclid.

The majority of the park is partially-shaded, mowed-grass green space. This expansive area is home to an 18-hole disc golf course. On the park's north, benches overlooking Lake Erie line the top of gently graded, partially mowed-grass, partially-vegetated, bluff. Wooden steps lead down the middle of the bluff to more than 1,100 feet of coastal access.

This beach is divided by a large groin and fishing pier near the eastern end. The 900-foot west beach area averages 120 feet wide. The foot-friendly sand at the back of the beach is mixed with small stones and shell fragments closer to the water. Three offshore breakwaters provide shore protection. Per city regulation, swimming and other forms of water contact are not permitted at Euclid's public beaches. The shore access east of the pier averages less than 30-feet wide. The upper park area here is heavily shaded.

Trails, some asphalt paved and some compacted gravel, weave throughout the park connecting various amenities including the beach, parking lots and playground. Additional amenities include a picnic pavilion and tables and the Albert W. Henn Mansion, which is listed on the National Register of Historic Places.

Field Notes:

_____

_____

_____

Amenities and Services:

Location Map:

Lake Erie

Sims Park
X

Euclid Park

Lakeshore

Lukart
Lake Edge
E. 233
E. 242
E. 238
E. 241
Sunnycliff
Buckner
Nobles Beach
E. 235
E. 232
E. 221
E. 228
E. 220
Bliss
283
Farringdon

Williams

0   850   1,700   2,550   3,400

Feet

Cuyahoga County

Date Visited: _____

Learn More:
City of Euclid
(216) 289-2700
www.cityofeuclid.com

Established: March 6, 1840
2000 Population: 227,511
2010 Projection: 233,890
Land Area and Rank: 228.2 square miles, 88 of 88
County Seat: City of Painesville
Named for: Lake Erie

Miles of Coast: 31 miles
Miles of Publicly Accessible Coast: 6.5 miles
Number of Access Sites: 27

Lake County

A brief history:

Lake County was formed on March 6, 1840, out of 228 square miles formerly comprising the northern townships of Geauga County. Lake County has the smallest land area of Ohio's 88 counties but has recently experienced significant population growth and ranks 11th among all Ohio counties. The city of Painesville is the county seat; Mentor is the largest city.

Lake County's name is derived from its location on the shore of Lake Erie. Many of the county's early residents were Mormon, who established Kirtland Temple in the 1830s. Although many Mormons eventually relocated from Ohio, the Kirtland Temple is a National Historic Landmark and today has a visitors center museum. Lake County also has a rich history of having actively participated in the Underground Railroad, which facilitated the transport of slaves to freedom. Other monuments and landmarks in the county include Holden Arboretum, one of the largest arboretums and botanical gardens in the United States, and the President James A. Garfield National Historic Site.

Lake County is predominantly rural and maintains vibrant nursery and winery industries. Approximately one-third of Ohio's nursery stock is grown here. The majority of county residents earn their living by working in manufacturing, sales or service positions. The Grand River and Chagrin River, both important Lake Erie tributaries and designated State Scenic Rivers, provide the county with many economic and recreational opportunities.

Learn More:

Lake County
www.lakecountyohio.org

City of Eastlake
www.eastlakeohio.com

City of Mentor
cityofmentor.com

City of Mentor-on-the-Lake
www.citymol.org

City of Wickliffe
www.cityofwillowick.com

City of Willoughby
www.willoughbyohio.com

Lake County Chamber of Commerce
www.lakecountychambers.com

Lake County Port Authority
www.lcedc.org

Lake County Visitors Bureau
www.lakevisit.com

Lake Metroparks
www.lakemetroparks.com

Mentor Area Chamber of Commerce
www.mentorchamber.org

Painesville Area Chamber of Commerce
www.painesvilleohchamber.org

Painesville Township
www.pvilletwp.com

Village of Fairport Harbor
www.fairportharbor.org

Western Lake County Chamber of Commerce
www.wlcacc.com

Willoughby Area Chamber of Commerce
www.willoughbyareachamber.com

Public Access Management:

Local	17
Metropark	5
Port Authority	2
State	2

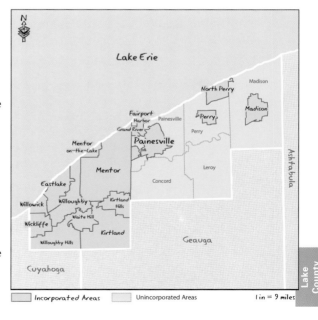

Willowick Lakefront

Location:
Lake Shore Boulevard
(SR 283) at
East 305th Street
Willowick, OH

Lat/Long (Hall):
N 41° 38.41'
W 081° 28.55'

Lat/Long (Park):
N 41° 38.42'
W 081° 28.42'

Waterbody:
Lake Erie

**Access
Site Type:**
Scenic

Environments:
Bluff
Rocky Shore
Sandy Beach
Manmade Shore

Lake
County

The 10 acres surrounding Willowick's City Hall Complex consist of two adjacent coastal access sites; a scenic overlook to the north and Willowick Lakefront Park to the east (managed by Lake Metroparks). The parking areas for the two access sites are both north of State Route 283 (Lake Shore Boulevard) near the three-way intersection with East 305th Street and Bayridge Road.

The park is partially-shaded mowed-grass with picnic tables and grills placed throughout. Park benches, a glider-style swing and a gazebo overlooking Lake Erie atop a 30-foot high, steeply graded bluff.

To control bluff erosion, the ODNR Division of Soil and Water Conservation partnered with the Sam Wharram Nature Club to plant native prairie flowering plants and grasses. Additional shore protection includes nearly 80 cement blocks similar to highway dividers which are placed in a stepped pattern parallel to shore down the middle of the beach. The 580-foot long beach is comprised of large-grain sand which is heavily mixed with varying sizes and types of stones and rocks. Due to submerged hazards, swimming and wading are prohibited.

Additional amenities include the Lakefront Lodge which was once a private residence. This rentable building is used to host public recreation programs and also houses Lake Metroparks' Volunteer Department.

Pets must be leashed and alcohol is prohibited.

Park and City Hall

Amenities and Services (Hall):

Amenities and Services (Park):

Location Map:

1 – Willowick City Hall Scenic Access
2 – Willowick Lakefront Park
    "Lakefront Lodge"

Lake Erie

Lake Shore

Vine — 640

E. 314

E. 312

Bayridge

E. 310

E. 309

E. 308

E. 307

283

E. 305

Cresthaven

Bruce

Sylvan

Fairway

Clarmont

Willowick

0   850   1,700   2,550   3,400
Feet

Field Notes:

_____

_____

_____

_____

_____

_____

_____

_____

_____

_____

_____

_____

_____

_____

Date Visited: _____

Lake County

Learn More:
Lake Metroparks
(440) 639-7275
www.lakemetroparks.com
or
City of Willowick
www.cityofwillowick.com

Quentin Road Pa

Location:
Lake Shore Boulevard
(SR 283) at
Quentin Road
Eastlake, OH

Latitude:
N 41° 39.29′

Longitude:
W 081° 27.56′

Waterbody:
Lake Erie

**Access
Site Type:**
Recreational

Environments:
Bluff

The 1.1-acre Quentin Road Park is north of State Route 283 (Lake Shore Boulevard) at the northwest corner of Quentin Road's northern terminus in the city of Eastlake. The small, unlined, asphalt parking lot is adjacent to the road with an old, tall pine tree and single story unsigned beige brick building at the lot's northeast side.

No signs denote Quentin Road Park as a public park; however its amenities imply such. They include swings, a tall metal slide, spring bounce animals, picnic tables and scenic benches overlooking Lake Erie. The mowed-grass grounds are flanked on both sides by deciduous trees.

A chain-link fence, with "No trespassing" signs, near the top of the bluff prohibits the public from accessing the bluff to the 105-foot long shore (same width as the upper park area). A small section north of the fence is mowed. The rest of the bluff is vegetated by natural plants.

Lake
County

...rk

Amenities and Services:

Location Map:

Lake Erie

283

Quentin Road Park

Roberts
Beachpark
Campers
Willowick
Stevens
Guilbert
Kenilworth
Rokeby
Mannering
Quentin
Waverly
Woodstock
Lake Shore
E. 331
E. 330
E. 329
E. 328
E. 332

0   850   1,700   2,550   3,400

Feet

Field Notes:

_____
_____
_____
_____
_____
_____
_____
_____
_____
_____
_____
_____
_____
_____
_____
_____
_____
_____
_____

Date Visited: _____

Learn More:
City of Eastlake
www.eastlakeohio.com

Lake
County

Eastlake Seawall

Location:
End of Erie Road, near
Halsey Drive
Eastlake, OH

Latitude:
N 41° 40.49′

Longitude:
W 081° 26.43′

Waterbody:
Lake Erie

**Access
Site Type:**
Recreational
Impervious
Pier

Environments:
Manmade Shore

Lake
County

The 0.9-acre Eastlake Seawall is at the northern terminus of Erie Road, which intersects State Route 283 (Lake Shore Boulevard) about one mile to the south.

The Eastlake Seawall is 960 feet west of the Chagrin River mouth and adjacent to the east of First Energy Corp.'s Eastlake Power Plant. The plant's warm water discharge into Lake Erie attracts fish and birds, especially during winter months when the rest of the lake freezes. Birds use the discharge area for feeding and bobbing in the water making this site a good winter bird watching location. Even in the coldest winters, the warm water opens a lead in the ice that lies within view of the seawall's parking lot.

Parking areas on the seawall are toward the south while the north and east sides of the manmade, asphalt covered bulkhead provide more than 500 feet of fishing access.

The majority of this site is paved impervious surface; however a small amount of green space is located on the south side of the parking lot. A few picnic tables are located here beneath deciduous trees.

Posted signs permit 24-hour fishing with a valid Ohio fishing license. Otherwise, the seawall is closed from 11 pm to 6 am. Signs also state that use of the seawall is free for city residents. During peak hours, a fee may be charged for non-Eastlake residents. Swimming and boat launching are prohibited.

Field Notes:

_____

_____

_____

_____

Amenities and Services:

_____

_____

_____

_____

_____

Location Map:

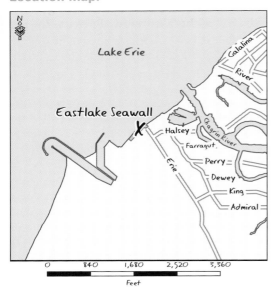

_____

_____

_____

_____

_____

_____

_____

_____

_____

_____

Date Visited: _____

Learn More:
City of Eastlake
www.eastlakeohio.com

Willowbeach Park

Location:
Lake Shore (SR 283)
and Traymore blvds.
Eastlake, OH

Latitude:
N 41° 41.32'

Longitude:
W 081° 24.91'

Waterbody:
Lake Erie

**Access
Site Type:**
Recreational

Environments:
Bluff

The 1.1-acre Willowbeach Park is north of State Route 283 (Lake Shore Boulevard) about 100 feet east of the Traymore Boulevard intersection. This coastal access site is east of the mouth of the Chagrin River on the city of Eastlake's east side.

Similar to Eastlake's Quentin Road Park on the city's west side, no signs denote Willowbeach as a public park. The parking lot is adjacent to the road and runs nearly the full 100-foot width of the park. The asphalt pavement continues north into a picnic pavilion with a round blue sign recognizing the Eastlake Police Athletic League.

A full-size basketball court, tall metal slide, two swing sets and a large sandbox round out the park's amenities.

The mowed-grass grounds are flanked on both sides by a chain-link fence. The fence runs north of park amenities at the top of a steep vegetated bluff. The fence prohibits shore access; there is no beach at the base of the bluff.

Picnic tables overlooking Lake Erie are placed just south of the fence. North of the fence, two tall deciduous trees as well as trees on neighboring private property, partially shade the park.

Willowbeach Park is a stop on the LakeTran Bus route.

Lake County

Field Notes:

_____

_____

_____

_____

_____

_____

_____

_____

Amenities and Services:

_____

_____

_____

_____

_____

Location Map:

N

283

Lake Erie

Christine

Willowbeach Park
X

Traymore
Willow
Paxton
Courtland
Plymouth
Shelton
Oxford
Green
Lake Shore
E. Overlook
St. Lawrence
Tam A Rac

| 0 | 850 | 1,700 | 2,550 | 3,400 |

Feet

_____

_____

_____

Date Visited: _____

Learn More:
City of Eastlake
www.eastlakeohio.com

Lake
County

Sunset Park

Location:
North Beachview
Road from Beachview
Road to Elmwood Dr.
Willoughby, OH

Latitude:
N 41° 41.84′

Longitude:
W 081° 24.19′

Waterbody:
Lake Erie

**Access
Site Type:**
Scenic

Environments:
Bluff
Manmade Shore

Lake
County

The 2-acre Sunset Park is a linear strip of green space north of North Beachview Road in the city of Willoughby. The park extends from Beachview Road on the west to the terminus of Elmwood Drive on the east. Both the road and the drive intersect State Route 283 (Lake Shore Boulevard), which is to the south.

Sunset Park is primarily a scenic overlook with picnic tables and swing benches overlooking Lake Erie atop a partially-mowed grass sloped bluff. The area of flat ground at the top of the bluff averages 20 feet wide along the park's 630-foot length.

Although very steep, one can traverse the smooth, manicured bluff that leads down to a concrete capped bulkhead. The top of the bulkhead is approximately 10 feet above the water level of Lake Erie. For safety purposes, a chain-rope barrier fence is placed on the lake side of the narrow cap which can serve as a walkway. Access beyond the fence down to a narrow pocket beach and the lake is prohibited. There are no signs prohibiting fishing.

Pull-off parking for Sunset Park is available north of North Beachview Road.

Field Notes:

_____

_____

_____

_____

_____

_____

_____

Amenities and Services:

_____

_____

Location Map:

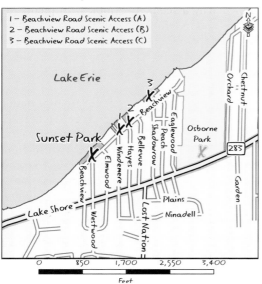

1 – Beachview Road Scenic Access (A)
2 – Beachview Road Scenic Access (B)
3 – Beachview Road Scenic Access (C)

Lake Erie

Sunset Park

Lake Shore

Osborne Park

283

_____

_____

_____

_____

_____

_____

_____

_____

Date Visited: _____

Learn More:
City of Willoughby
Parks and Recreation
(440) 953-4200
www.willoughbyohio.com

Lake County

Beachview Road

Waterbody:
Lake Erie

**Access
Site Type:**
Scenic

Environments:
Bluff

East of Sunset Park on North Beachview Road, three city-owned lots provide a combined 2 acres of public access. From east to west, they are referred in this document as Beachview Road Scenic Access "A," "B" and "C," respectively. None of the sites are signed; however, each site has a small open area of mowed-grass north of a wooden split-rail fence. Bench swings are located at sites "B" and "C" and a picnic table at site "C."

Location (A):
Beachview and
Windemere roads
Willoughby, OH

Lat/Long (A):
N 41° 41.92'
W 081° 24.07'

Location (B):
Beachview and
Hayes roads
Willoughby, OH

Lat/Long (B):
N 41° 41.95'
W 081° 24.02'

Location (C):
Beachview and
Shadowrow roads
Willoughby, OH

Lat/Long (C):
N 41° 42.01'
W 081° 23.92'

Lake
County

Scenic Accesses

Amenities and Services (A):

Amenities and Services (B):

Amenities and Services (C):

Location Map:

1 – Beachview Road Scenic Access (A)
2 – Beachview Road Scenic Access (B)
3 – Beachview Road Scenic Access (C)

Lake Erie

Sunset Park

Beachview

Osborne Park

Chestnut

Orchard

Eaglewood

Peach

Shadowrow

Bellevue

Hayes

Windemere

Elmwood

Beachview

Garden

283

Plains

Ninadell

Lake Shore

Westwood

Lost Nation

0   850   1,700   2,550   3,400

Feet

Field Notes:

_____
_____
_____
_____
_____
_____
_____
_____
_____
_____
_____
_____
_____

Date Visited: _____

Learn More:
City of Willoughby
Parks and Recreation
(440) 953-4200
www.willoughbyohio.com

Lake County

Osborne Park

Location:
Lake Shore Boulevard
(SR 283) and
Orchard Road
Willoughby, OH

Latitude:
N 41° 41.83'

Longitude:
W 081° 23.69'

Waterbody:
Lake Erie

**Access
Site Type:**
Recreational

Environments:
Bluff
Sandy Beach
Manmade Shore

The 43.3-acre Osborne Park is north of State Route 283 (Lake Shore Boulevard) between Eaglewood Drive and Orchard Road. On some maps, the park is listed as Willoughby Municipal Park.

A foot-traffic only access is available off Eaglewood Drive at the park's north end. Osborne's parking lot and various paved walkways extend into the park grounds from Lake Shore Boulevard. From the parking lot, a partially paved/partially gravel path leads toward Lake Erie. The path ends atop a gently sloping mowed-grass bluff that has been terraced into two tiers. The slope's horizontal plane is more than 200 feet for nearly the entire width of the park's 0.3-mile Lake Erie shore.

Depending on water levels, a narrow beach of gravel and large-grain sand mixed with various sizes and types of rocks may be present north of the precast concrete modules lining the base of the bluff. Benches, park swings, picnic tables and grills are spaced along the top of the bluff. A striking feature is a single, massive white oak tree (*Quercus alba*) with an 80-foot crown.

The majority of the park's land is un-shaded mowed-grass open space. A heavily wooded area is along the park's northwest side. Additional park amenities include an outdoor swimming pool with water slide, a rentable picnic pavilion, playground equipment, baseball, football and soccer fields, basketball, tennis and sand volleyball courts and a disc golf course.

The park closes at dusk.

Field Notes:

_____

_____

_____

_____

_____

_____

_____

_____

_____

_____

_____

_____

_____

_____

_____

_____

Amenities and Services:

Location Map:

Date Visited: _____

Learn More:
City of Willoughby
Parks and Recreation
(440) 953-4200
www.willoughbyohio.com

Overlook Beach P

Location:
Thunderbird Drive at
Reynolds Road
Mentor-on-the-Lake,
OH

Latitude:
N 41° 42.69′

Longitude:
W 081° 22.69′

Waterbody:
Lake Erie

**Access
Site Type:**
Recreational

Environments:
Bluff
Sandy Beach

The nearly 3-acre Overlook Beach Park is located in the city of Mentor-on-the-Lake. The parking lot is accessed off Thunderbird Drive, just west of the Reynolds Road intersection. Reynolds Road becomes Salida Road near the park's eastern boundary.

A paved path leads from the parking lot north to a wooden observation deck. This handicap-accessible deck has a staircase descending to the beach. A 2002, grant from the Ohio Coastal Management Program funded, in part, the deck construction project that created a safe beach access and corrected a surface water runoff problem that was causing erosion.

The park's 375-foot long, 50-foot wide beach consists of foot-friendly sand that is mixed with small stones and shell fragments closer to the water's edge. A storm water outfall crosses the beach at the western end. The east end of the beach is marked with a stone revetment.

Additional amenities at Overlook Beach Park include a picnic area, playground equipment, a basketball court and picnic gazebo with additional picnic tables placed throughout the park. The western two-thirds of the park is mostly unshaded, mowed-grass open space; the eastern portion has a thick deciduous tree canopy.

Lake
County

ark

Amenities and Services:

Location Map:

N

Lake Erie

Salida

Overlook
Beach Park
X

Melody
Lake
Pinehurst
Holly
Miami
Southland

Shamrock

Wedgewood
Reynolds
Fern
Larkspur
Goldenrod

Goldenrod
Primrose

Campbell
Dahlia
Manor

Thunderbird
Maplewood
Firwood
Cedarwood

0   850   1,700   2,550   3,400

Feet

Field Notes:

_____

_____

_____

_____

_____

_____

_____

_____

_____

_____

_____

_____

_____

_____

_____

_____

_____

Date Visited: _____

Lake
County

Learn More:
City of Mentor-on-the-Lake
(440) 257-7216
www.citymol.org

Mentor Beach Pa

Location:
Lakeshore Boulevard
(SR 283) and Andrews
Road (SR 283)
Mentor-on-the-Lake,
OH

Latitude:
N 41° 43.2'

Longitude:
W 081° 21.68'

Waterbody:
Lake Erie

**Access
Site Type:**
Recreational

Environments:
Bluff
Sandy Beach
Manmade Shore

Lake
County

The 9.1-acre Mentor Beach Park is at the northern terminus of Andrews Road where it intersects with Twilight Drive (on the west) and Lakeshore Boulevard (on the east). State Route 283 follows both Andrews Road and Lakeshore Boulevard.

While the park is located in the city of Mentor-on-the-Lake, the city of Mentor owns and maintains the park which includes a two-story, lakefront pavilion available for rent. Additional amenities include picnic areas, playground equipment and a soccer field. Aside from this sport field, the mowed-grass park grounds are mostly shaded by deciduous trees.

The park's 0.2-mile Lake Erie shore can be accessed via a path down vegetated slope on the east side of the park. Shore access is also provided next to the pavilion via a stairway. Along with a landing and promenade built in 1999, the stairway's construction was funded in part with a grant from the Ohio Coastal Management Program.

The park's entire shore is armored for erosion protection. The park's western beach area is enclosed, separated from the open lake water by a manmade wall. Swimming here is prohibited. Depending on water levels, a beach may be present on the park's east side, lakeward of a stone revetment.

...rk

Amenities and Services:

Location Map:

Lake Erie

Mentor Beach Park

Field Notes:

_____

_____

_____

_____

_____

_____

_____

_____

_____

_____

_____

_____

_____

_____

_____

_____

_____

_____

Date Visited: _____

Learn More:
City of Mentor
Parks and Recreation
(440) 974-5720
www.cityofmentor.com

Mentor Lagoons Natu

Location:
8365 Harbor Drive
Harbor Drive north
of Lakeshore
Boulevard (SR 283)
Mentor, OH

Latitude:
N 41° 43.59'

Longitude:
W 081° 20.29'

Waterbody:
Lake Erie

**Access
Site Type:**
Natural

Environments:
Bluff
Sandy Beach
Wetland

Lake County

The 450-acre Mentor Lagoons Nature Preserve and Marina is at the northern terminus of Harbor Drive which intersects State Route 283 (Lakeshore Boulevard).

The preserve boasts a 1.5-mile "wild," non-swimming beach and more than 3 miles of foot and bike trails that encircle the preserve. The trails link to those in the 691-acre Mentor Marsh State Nature Preserve which is jointly owned and managed by ODNR and the Cleveland Museum of Natural History, the latter operates an on-site visitor center.

The city of Mentor-owned lagoons preserve is north and east of the state preserve; the two preserves' history and the natural resources they protect are unified. Designated as a National Natural Landmark in 1966, Mentor Marsh occupies an ancient, abandoned Grand River channel which today is one of the largest remaining natural Lake Erie marshes. The preserves encompass nearly all of the riverine marsh wetlands. Additional environs include rare dunes, beech-sugar maple forests, mixed oak swamp forests and mature oak bluffs. The preserves are an important breeding and nursery area for fish and waterfowl and provide a resting place for annual migrations of neo-tropical birds and butterflies.

Adjacent to the west of the preserves is the city-owned, 500-wet slip Mentor Lagoons Marina with seasonal and transient dockage. Charges for marina services may differ for city and non-city residents.

Trail signs are posted throughout the preserve. Maps are available at the marina office and trailhead. Physically challenged visitors may request use of electric carts to access the trails by calling 440-205-3625 before visiting. Preserve hours are dawn to dusk year-round.

e Preserve and Marina

Amenities and Services:

Location Map:

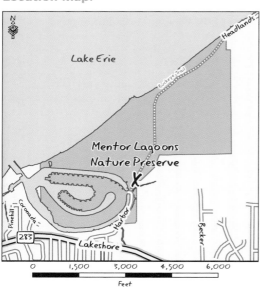

Lake Erie

Buckeye Trail

Headlands

Mentor Lagoons
Nature Preserve

X

Pinehill

Coronada

283

Harbor

Lakeshore

Becker

| 0 | 1,500 | 3,000 | 4,500 | 6,000 |

Feet

Field Notes:

_____

_____

_____

_____

_____

_____

_____

_____

_____

_____

_____

_____

_____

_____

_____

_____

_____

Date Visited: _____

Learn More:
City of Mentor
Parks and Recreation
(440) 974-5720
www.cityofmentor.com

Headlands Beach

Location:
Heisley (SR 44) and
Headlands roads
Painesville Township,
OH

Latitude:
N 41° 45.17'

Longitude:
W 081° 17.30'

Waterbody:
Lake Erie

**Access
Site Type:**
Recreational

Environments:
Sandy Beach

The 122.7-acre Headlands Beach State Park is at the northern terminus of State Route 44 (Heisley Road) at the Headlands Road/Williams Street intersection west of the Grand River in Fairport Harbor.

Headlands boasts the longest natural swimming beach in Ohio. The beach's publicly accessible portion is 0.6 miles long and 200 feet wide on the western end expanding to nearly 500 feet wide on the park's east side. To the east, the state park is adjacent to Headlands Dunes State Nature Preserve. Combined, the park and preserve shore lengths create more than 1-mile of walkable coast.

The foot-friendly sand is very fine in the back beach and increases in size closer to the water's edge; the closest 20 feet is comprised of large-grain sand heavily mixed with various types and sizes pebbles and stones. Low dunes and deciduous trees line the southern edge of the beach. Parking is available to the south.

An asphalt-paved bike and walking trail runs the park's length providing access to the bathhouses, concession stands, picnic shelters, tables, grills and playground equipment located in the parking area.

During summer, the beach is groomed and lifeguards are on duty. At times, large waves develop (*see beach safety tips in the introduction*). Only U.S. Coast Guard-approved flotation devices may be used at the beach. Pets are prohibited. The park is open year-round and closes 30 minutes after sunset.

The statewide Buckeye Trail's northern terminus is at Headlands Beach. The park is also adjacent to the north of Mentor Marsh State Nature Preserve's eastern reaches.

State Park

Amenities and Services:

Location Map:

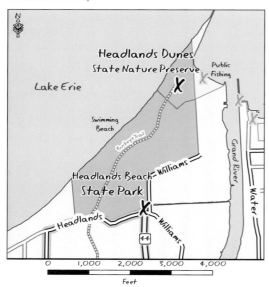

Headlands Dunes
State Nature Preserve

Public Fishing

Lake Erie

Swimming Beach

Buckeye Trail

Grand River

Water

Headlands Beach Williams
State Park

Headlands

Williams

44

0   1,000   2,000   3,000   4,000

Feet

Field Notes:

_____

_____

_____

_____

_____

_____

_____

_____

_____

_____

_____

_____

_____

_____

_____

_____

_____

_____

Date Visited: _____

Lake County

Learn More:
ODNR Division of Parks and Recreation
Contact: Cleveland Lakefront State Park
(216) 881-8141
ohiodnr.com/parks
ohiodnr.com/tabid/742/default.aspx

Headlands Dunes S

Location:
Heisley (SR 44) and
Headlands roads
Painesville Township,
OH

Latitude:
N 41° 45.68'

Longitude:
W 081° 17.11'

Waterbody:
Lake Erie

**Access
Site Type:**
Natural

Environments:
Dunes
Sandy Beach

**Lake
County**

Ohio's premier example of coastal dunes is Headlands Dunes State Nature Preserve located at the northern terminus of State Route 44 (Heisley Road) at the Headlands Road and Williams Street intersection.

Headlands is located just west of the Grand River's 3,878-foot West Breakwater. The breakwater has resulted in the preserve's growth since ODNR acquired the original 16 acres in 1976. The breakwater impedes the natural, eastward movement of sand along the coast. Sand becomes impounded on the structure's west side, and the preserve has grown to an estimated 24 acres. This does not account for the volume of sand that has accumulated in the ever-taller dunes.

A dune's vertical growth occurs as wind blows sand and deposits it into the crowns of switchgrass and beach grass plants. The plants grow vertically through the sand, spreading into huge root-like mats. This process stabilizes the dunes to varying degrees and leads to the establishment of additional highly specialized dune vegetation.

Headlands is an excellent site for viewing migrating birds and butterflies. Self-guided trails provide visitors with access through the dunes; one trail leads to the adjacent Fairport Harbor West Breakwater and Lighthouse. Some dunes are fenced off to prevent access as dunes are fragile, easily destroyed environments.

The Buckeye Trail's northern terminus is adjacent to the dune trail entrance. Preserve parking is in the low-numbered lots at the adjoining Headlands Beach State Park. Combined, the park's and preserve's shore lengths account for more than 1 mile of walkable coast.

...te Nature Preserve

Amenities and Services:

Field Notes:

_____
_____
_____
_____
_____
_____
_____
_____
_____
_____
_____
_____
_____
_____
_____
_____
_____

Location Map:

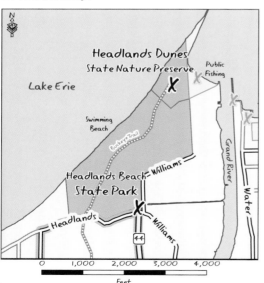

N

Headlands Dunes
State Nature Preserve

Public Fishing

Lake Erie

Swimming Beach

Buckeye Trail

Headlands Beach—Williams
State Park

Grand River

Water

Headlands

Williams

44

0   1,000   2,000   3,000   4,000
Feet

Date Visited: _____

Learn More:
ODNR
Division of Natural Areas and Preserves
ohiodnr.com/dnap
ohiodnr.com/tabid/892/default.aspx

Lake County

Fairport Harbor W

Location:
Heisley (SR 44) and
Headlands roads
Painesville Township,
OH

Latitude:
N 41° 45.70'

Longitude:
W 081° 16.97'

Waterbody:
Lake Erie
Grand River

**Access
Site Type:**
Impervious
Pier

Environments:
Riparian/River
Manmade Shore

Lake
County

The Fairport Harbor West Breakwater is adjacent to Headlands Dunes State Nature Preserve and accessible from the nature preserve via a marked trail. Breakwater parking is in the low-numbered lots at the adjoining Headlands Beach State Park, at the north terminus of State Route 44 (Heisley Road).

About two-thirds of the 3,878-foot long West Breakwater is covered by impounded sand. Fishing is allowed from the breakwater, which is comprised of large limestone blocks and a steel sheet-pile bulkhead. The highly photographed, 42-foot tall Fairport Harbor West Breakwater Light, which has an attached white brick two-story keeper's cottage, stands 540 feet from the breakwater's north end.

The steel-framed brick West Breakwater Light was erected in 1925. The original fourth order Fresnel lens flashed a white light, three seconds on and three seconds off. When the Fairport Harbor Breakwater Light was automated, the Fresnel lens was replaced with a 300-millimeter acrylic lens.

The U.S. Coast Guard maintains the light as a navigational aid; the lighthouse itself is privately owned, while the underlying navigational structure is owned by the U.S. Army Corps of Engineers. The able-footed can walk out to and around the lighthouse to the end of the breakwater.

‥st Breakwater

Amenities and Services:

Field Notes:

_____
_____
_____
_____
_____
_____
_____
_____
_____
_____
_____
_____
_____
_____
_____

Location Map:

1 – Fairport Harbor West Breakwater
2 – Fairport Harbor Short Pier
3 – Fairport Harbor Port Authority Boat Access

Lake Erie

Headlands Dunes State Nature Preserve

Public Fishing

Fishing Pier

Fairport Harbor Lakefront Park

Headlands Beach State Park

Grand River

Water

Williams

2nd

High

Eagle

Plum

3rd

Vine

| 0 | 850 | 1,700 | 2,550 | 3,400 |

Feet

Lake County

Date Visited: _____

Learn More:
U.S. Coast Guard - Light Station Information
uscg.mil/history/weblighthouses/LHOH.asp
U.S. Army Corps of Engineers -
Detroit District
www.lre.usace.army.mil

Fairport Harbor
Short Pier and Port

Location:
Water and Second st.
Fairport Harbor, OH

Lat/Long (Pier):
N 41° 45.61'
W 081° 16.79'

Lat/Long (Access):
N 41° 45.53'
W 081° 16.71'

Waterbody:
Lake Erie
Grand River

**Access
Site Type:**
Impervious
Pier
Recreational

Environments:
Riparian/River
Manmade Shore
Sandy Beach

Lake
County

Two public access sites are just east of the Grand River mouth in Fairport Harbor.

The parking area for the 2.4-acre Fairport Harbor Port Authority Boat Access is at the northern terminus of Water Street, north of the Second Street intersection. There is a small fee for parking at the paved site and another fee for launching boats on one of the four lanes. Foot access to the site is free. The boat access is partially shaded with the 0.75 acres along the site's east side offering a small beach area and picnic tables. Fishing and swimming are not permitted.

A 435-foot concrete walkway extends from the parking lot at the Fairport Harbor Port Authority Boat Access and leads to the Fairport Harbor Short Pier. The handicap-accessible, paved concrete pier extends 590 feet into the protected harbor waters. There is no signage recognizing the pier as public. Signs signifying the private dock property west of the walkway read "No Trespassing."

The Fairport Harbor Port Authority Boat Access site is adjacent to the west of Fairport Harbor Lakefront Park.

Authority Boat Access

Amenities and Services (Pier):

Amenities and Services (Access):

Location Map:

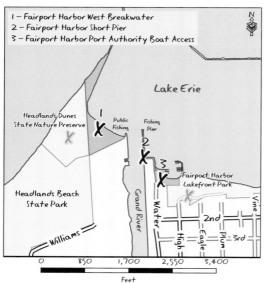

1 – Fairport Harbor West Breakwater
2 – Fairport Harbor Short Pier
3 – Fairport Harbor Port Authority Boat Access

Lake Erie

Headlands Dunes State Nature Preserve

Public Fishing

Fishing Pier

Headlands Beach State Park

Fairport Harbor Lakefront Park

Grand River

Water

Williams

2nd

High

Eagle

Plum

3rd

Vine

0   850   1,700   2,550   3,400

Feet

Field Notes:

Date Visited: _____

Learn More:
Fairport Harbor Port Authority
(440) 357-8466
www.fairportharbor.org

Lake County

Fairport Harbor

Location:
301 Huntington Beach
Drive
High and
Second streets
Fairport Harbor, OH

Latitude:
N 41° 45.48'

Longitude:
W 081° 16.60'

Waterbody:
Lake Erie

**Access
Site Type:**
Recreational

Environments:
Bluff
Sandy Beach

Lake
County

Along a 0.45-mile stretch of Lake Erie shore, the 21-acre Fairport Harbor Lakefront Park is east of the Grand River mouth. Parking is available in a large lot on Huntington Beach Drive at the northern terminus of High Street, north Additional beach access for foot and bike traffic is at the northern termini of East and Vine streets.

Owned by the village of Fairport Harbor and managed by the Lake Metroparks, the site features walking paths that link various amenities throughout the park. From the west end of the park a foot-friendly groomed sand beach extends 1,330 feet east. The beach ranges from 140- to 180-feet wide and narrows at the park's east end where the shore is armored.

Additional amenities at the back of the beach include picnic tables, playground equipment, a concession stand, a kayak rental booth, beach volleyball courts and a bathhouse. Along the park's south, a narrow tree-lined green space runs the length of the site. On the west, the green space expands south into a 3.5-acre open mowed-grass field with a small amphitheater. Adjacent to the south, the historic Fairport Harbor Lighthouse and Marine Museum is at the northwest corner of High and Second streets.

Lakefront Park is adjacent to the east of the Fairport Harbor Port Authority's Boat Access, which has a 425-foot pier with transient dockage.

Lakefront Park

Amenities and Services:

Field Notes:

_____
_____
_____
_____
_____
_____
_____
_____
_____
_____
_____
_____
_____
_____

Date Visited: _____

Location Map:

Lake Erie

Fairport Harbor
Short Pier

Fairport Harbor
Lakefront Park

Grand River

2nd

3rd

High
Eagle
Plum
Vine
Chestnut
East
Water
4th
New 4th
5th

535

0   850   1,700   2,550   3,400

Feet

Learn More:
Lake Metroparks
(440) 639-7275
www.lakemetroparks.com

Lake County

Painesville Townsh

Location:
1025 Hardy Road
Hardy and Lake roads
Painesville Township,
OH

Latitude:
N 41° 46.00′

Longitude:
W 081° 13.91′

Waterbody:
Lake Erie

**Access
Site Type:**
Recreational

Environments:
Bluff
Manmade Shore

The 37-acre Painesville Township Park is on the west side of Hardy Road a half-mile north of its intersection with State Route 535 (Fairport Nursery Road).

The park was established in the early 1920s as a popular recreational area offering baseball fields, a dance hall, picnic areas, an open-air pavilion and a beach. Over time, shore erosion has claimed the beach and pavilion. Painesville Township Park includes five regulation softball fields and a handicap-accessible, rentable hall with a 5,000 square-foot wooden dance floor.

The park's 1,637-foot long shore is partially shaded with deciduous trees. Benches overlooking Lake Erie are spaced behind a wooden split-rail fence that runs the length of the park separating the upper park from a bluff. A gently graded gravel pathway leads from the upper park down the shaded natural bluff to the portion of the bluff that has been re-graded and planted with grass and native vegetation. A 10-foot tall bulkhead capped with a steel railing prevents direct lake access for safety reasons.

Lake Metroparks has managed the township-owned property since 1991. Additional amenities include picnic tables, playground equipment, concessions and restrooms. Swimming is prohibited.

p Park

Amenities and Services:

Location Map:

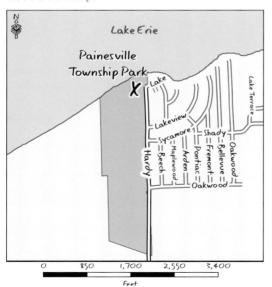

Field Notes:

_____
_____
_____
_____
_____
_____
_____
_____
_____
_____
_____
_____
_____
_____
_____
_____
_____
_____

Date Visited: _____

Learn More:
Lake Metroparks
(440) 639-7275
www.lakemetroparks.com

Perry Township P

Location:
Perry Park and
Parmly roads
Perry Township, OH

Latitude:
N 41° 47.66′

Longitude:
W 081° 09.82′

Waterbody:
Lake Erie

**Access
Site Type:**
Recreational

Environments:
Bluff
Sandy Beach
Manmade Shore

The L-shaped 70.4-acre Perry Township Park is north of Parmly Road along the west and east sides of the northern terminus of Perry Park Road.

At the park's west, a trail cuts through the steep bluff and leads down to a 900-foot narrow sand beach. The upland park area here is occupied by ball fields, parking, the Perry Township Community Center and open green space.

To the east of Perry Road, the north parking area overlooks Lake Erie from behind a wooden split-rail fence. Lakeward of the fence, a 125-foot wide mowed-grass, graded slope leads down to the park's 780-foot long stepped seawall made of precast concrete modules. There is no beach along this nearshore area which has submerged hazards including exposed rebar.

Use of the boat launch east of the seawall is limited to Perry Township residents and those camping in the park's 30 heavily-wood acres along the park's east. East of the boat ramp, a small tributary cuts through the bluff across an unguarded, 1,180-foot long swimming beach. The beach is is comprised of a mixture of stones, sand and shell fragments. The beach is backed by 30-foot, vertical, clay/glacial till bluff.

Park amenities include a picnic shelter, playground, concession stand, and athletic fields. General park hours are one-half hour before sunrise to one-half hour after sunset. As of March 2010, Perry Township is planning and seeking funding for park improvements, including extensive beach renovation.

ark

Amenities and Services:

Location Map:

Lake Erie

Perry Township Park

Parmly

Perry Park

| 0 | 850 | 1,700 | 2,550 | 3,400 |

Feet

Field Notes:

_____

_____

_____

_____

_____

_____

_____

_____

_____

_____

_____

_____

_____

_____

_____

_____

_____

_____

Date Visited: _____

Lake County

Learn More:
Perry Township Park
(440) 259-5957
www.perrytownship-lake.com

North Perry Vill

The 4.4-acre North Perry Village Park is on Lockwood Road about a half-mile west of the Antioch Road intersection and 0.65 miles east of First Energy Corp.'s Perry Nuclear Power Plant.

The park grounds include the North Perry Village Hall, police and zoning departments. A looping access road provides entry into the park from Lockwood Road. A second entrance is on the park's east side near the Hemlock Road intersection and adjacent to the park's playground equipment.

North Perry Village Park includes two picnic shelters, one of which is at the top of the bluff and overlooks the park's 320-foot shore. The vegetated bluff is flanked on each end with deciduous trees. A wooden split-rail fence along the bluff's length marks the boundary of parkland open to the public; use of the bluff north of the fence line and direct access to Lake Erie is prohibited due to unsafe conditions caused by the unstable bluff.

The majority of the park is comprised of mowed-grass open areas with a few trees planted throughout. Additional park amenities include a baseball field, grills and picnic tables.

Lake
County

ge Park

Amenities and Services:

Location Map:

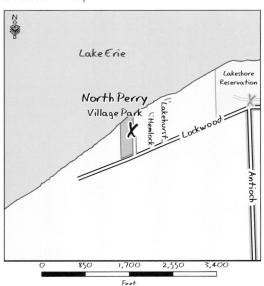

N

Lake Erie

Lakeshore
Reservation

North Perry
Village Park

Hemlock

Lakehurst

Lockwood

Antioch

X

0   850   1,700   2,550   3,400

Feet

Field Notes:

_____

_____

_____

_____

_____

_____

_____

_____

_____

_____

_____

_____

_____

_____

_____

_____

_____

Date Visited: _____

Learn More:
Village of North Perry
(440) 259-4994
www.northperry.org

Lake
County

Lakeshore Reserv

Location:
Lockwood and
Antioch roads
4799 Lockwood Road
North Perry, OH

Latitude:
N 41° 48.68'

Longitude:
W 081° 07.28'

Waterbody:
Lake Erie

**Access
Site Type:**
Recreational
Natural

Environments:
Bluff
Sandy Beach

Lake
County

The 84-acre Lakeshore Reservation is a Lake Metroparks facility fronting a half-mile of Lockwood Road. The park's access is at the northern terminus of Antioch Road in the village of North Perry.

Access to the park's 0.52-mile "wild" beach is provided via two sets of stairs leading down the heavily wooded bluff. The stairs, one located near the western one-third of shore and the other near the eastern park boundary, are accessible by way of a 1.6-mile network of handicap-accessible paved asphalt trails that meander throughout the park connecting various amenities.

The 10 parcels of land that comprise the park were purchased between 1967 and 1973. In some areas, previous owners planted non-native ornamental trees and shrubs amidst the native trees, including a large number of rhododendrons near the east boundary of the park.

Lakeshore Reservation is heavily wooded with just a few open mowed-grass areas near the parking lots. The park is home to the Strock Sculpture Garden, a memorial to Luanna Strock, wife of the park system's first naturalist, Don Strock. The memorial includes a sculpted sundial, a cable bridge and a bronze cast of the area.

Additional park amenities include two picnic shelters (one is first-come, first-served and the other may be reserved) and handicap-accessible restrooms. Fishing is permitted along the shore. A trail map is available at park kiosks and online.

ation

Amenities and Services:

Location Map:

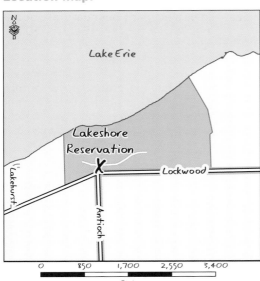

Lake Erie

Lakeshore
Reservation

Lakehurst

Lockwood

Antioch

N

0   850   1,700   2,550   3,400
Feet

Field Notes:

_____

_____

_____

_____

_____

_____

_____

_____

_____

_____

_____

_____

_____

_____

_____

_____

Date Visited: _____

Learn More:
Lake Metroparks
(440) 639-7275
www.lakemetroparks.com

Lake
County

Bill Stanton Comr

Location:
Chapel and
McMackin roads
5585 Chapel Road
Madison Township,
OH

Latitude:
N 41° 49.34'

Longitude:
W 081° 05.44'

Waterbody:
Lake Erie

**Access
Site Type:**
Recreational

Environments:
Bluff
Sandy Beach

Lake
County

The 32.8-acre Bill Stanton Community Park is along the north side of Chapel Road between McMackin and Haines roads in Madison Township.

The park includes a 0.2-mile shore. The western half of the park's shore is a nearly vertical, heavily vegetated bluff. A mixture of deciduous and evergreen trees grow along the bluff face and extend inland about 100 feet to create a small woods. There are no safe paths to traverse this nearly vertical extent of the bluff.

Along the park's east, a packed-dirt path zigzags down a graded, vegetated bluff to a wooden staircase which drops down to a 475-foot long beach. This natural sand beach is mixed with pebbles, small stones and shell fragments in larger quantities closer to the water's edge. Swimming, at one's own risk, is permitted.

Bill Stanton Community Park was established in 1999 and features many recreational amenities, including picnic facilities and grills, playground equipment, concessions, basketball and tennis courts and expansive mowed-grass areas, some of which are marked as soccer fields. The park also has various buildings available for rent including a banquet hall, recreation hall, chapel and cabin.

Dogs are the only pets allowed in the park; they must be leashed. The park closes at dusk, except during special events.

...unity Park

Field Notes:

Amenities and Services:

Location Map:

Lake Erie

Bill Stanton
Community Park
X

Chapel

Lake Overlook

McMackin

W. Tuttle Park

Fishermans Trail

Haines

Haines

| 0 | 850 | 1,700 | 2,550 | 3,400 |

Feet

Date Visited: _____

Learn More:
Madison Township
(440) 428-5128
www.madisontownship.net

Lake
County

Tuttle Park

Location:
West Tuttle Park Road
and Northway Drive
5825 Northway Drive
Madison Township,
OH

Latitude:
N 41° 49.52′

Longitude:
W 081° 04.90′

Waterbody:
Lake Erie

**Access
Site Type:**
Recreational

Environments:
Bluff
Sandy Beach

Lake County

The 7.9-acre Tuttle Park is between West Tuttle and East Tuttle roads in Madison Township. Parkland is both north and south of Northway Drive. Both Tuttle roads intersect Homestead Road to the south, which intersects Chapel Road at two locations.

The park's land north of Northway Drive includes a large stand of evergreen trees with deciduous trees lining the top of the bluff. Portions of the bluff are fenced to prohibit people from descending steeper areas. Graded portions of the bluff include a mixture of vegetation and mowed-grass and lead down to a 365-foot long shore. Concrete steps are located along the park's eastern boundary while the western area includes a steel staircase.

Swimming at one's own risk is permitted at the beach which includes five groins extending into Lake Erie. While the beach is comprised of sand mixed with pebbles and small stones perfect for skipping, caution should be taken as it also has irregular chunks of concrete rubble, some of which have exposed rebar.

Tuttle Park's upper shore area has a picnic pavilion and playground equipment. South of Northway Drive, park amenities include parking, baseball field and basketball and tennis courts.

Field Notes:

_____
_____
_____
_____
_____
_____
_____
_____
_____
_____
_____
_____
_____
_____
_____
_____
_____
_____
_____
_____

Amenities and Services:

Location Map:

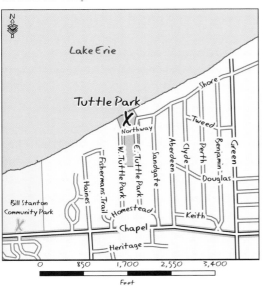

N

Lake Erie

Tuttle Park
X
Shore
Tweed
Northway
Green
Benjamin
Perth
Clyde
Aberdeen
Sandgate
W. Tuttle Park
E. Tuttle Park
Fisherman's Trail
Haines
Douglas
Homestead
Keith
Bill Stanton
Community Park
X
Chapel
Heritage

0   850   1,700   2,550   3,400
Feet

Date Visited: _____

Learn More:
Madison Township
(440) 428-5128
www.madisontownship.net

Lake County

Madison Township

Location:
Lake and
Hubbard roads
6717 Lake Road
Madison Township,
OH

Latitude:
N 41° 50.20'

Longitude:
W 081° 02.81'

Waterbody:
Lake Erie

**Access
Site Type:**
Recreational

Environments:
Bluff
Sandy Beach

Lake
County

The 11.9-acre Madison Township Park is at the northeast corner of Lake and Hubbard roads in Madison Township. The boat-trailer parking area is accessed at Parkview Drive's intersection with Lake Road East. Additional parking is adjacent to the road along the park's outer perimeter.

The park includes a 630-foot long beach comprised of medium- to large-grain sand mixed with small amounts of pebbles. The beach, wider at its western end, ranges from 60 to 75-feet wide. While popular for swimming, this beach has a variety of shore structures including groins and precast concrete modules that run the length of the shore. Madison Township officials have secured funding for beach improvements planned for late-summer 2010. The plans include removal of existing concrete structures and installation of offshore breakwaters.

Fishing is allowed along the shore and from the structures.

In the upper park, a wood fence marks the top of the tree-lined bluff along the western portion. A paved walkway extends from the north end of the parking area beside Hubbard Road, along the top of the bluff to a large picnic pavilion overlooking Lake Erie, which is in the middle of the park. North of the pavilion, a path leads down a graded, grass-covered bluff. The park's eastern end includes a looped drive and a small boat launch.

Additional amenities at Madison Township Park include a lighted baseball field, playground equipment, a basketball court and benches overlooking Lake Erie.

Park

Amenities and Services:

Location Map:

Field Notes:

_____
_____
_____
_____
_____
_____
_____
_____
_____
_____
_____
_____
_____
_____
_____
_____
_____
_____
_____

Date Visited: _____

Learn More:
Madison Township
(440) 428-5128
www.madisontownship.net

Arcola Creek Park

Location:
Dock Road at
Lakeshore Boulevard
941 Dock Road
Madison Township,
OH

Latitude:
N 41° 50.93'

Longitude:
W 081° 00.46'

Waterbody:
Lake Erie
Arcola Creek

**Access
Site Type:**
Natural

Environments:
Riparian/River
Estuarine
Sandy Beach
Wetland

Lake County

The 153-acre Arcola Creek Park is accessed from Dock Road one half-mile north of Lake Road in the northeastern-most corner of Lake County. The estuary and surrounding area has been restored to a natural condition from its early 1800s industrial past, which included being a shipping channel for the former town of Ellensburg.

An estuary is a partially enclosed body of water near a river or stream mouth where water flowing from the tributary meets and mixes with the water of a lake or ocean. In this case, water from Lake Erie spills into the estuary and mixes with the flowing waters of Arcola Creek.

The preserve's 0.1-mile shore is accessed via the Wick-ert Trail, a packed gravel path leading from the parking lot along the west side of the creek, through a line of de-ciduous trees and onto the beach. The fine-grained sand is heavily mixed with various types and sizes of smooth stones. Arcola Creek's mouth cuts through the beach near the preserve's eastern boundary. A small groin is near the beach's west end. Fishing in Lake Erie is permitted.

An observation deck near the south end of the trail pro-vides views of the wetlands which support a diverse num-ber of aquatic and terrestrial plant and animal species. Ar-cola Creek is also an important breeding area for fish and a frequent stopover for migrating birds. Managed by the Lake Metroparks, protection of Arcola Creek is also pro-vided by The Nature Conservancy, the Cleveland Museum of Natural History, the Friends of Arcola Creek and the Lake County Commissioners.

Field Notes:

Amenities and Services:

Location Map:

_____

_____

_____

_____

_____

_____

_____

_____

_____

_____

_____

_____

_____

_____

_____

_____

_____

_____

_____

_____

Date Visited: _____

Learn More:
Lake Metroparks
(440) 639-7275
www.lakemetroparks.com

Lake County

Established: February 10, 1807
2000 Population: 102,728
2010 Projection: 104,970
Land Area and Rank: 702.7 square miles, 1 of 88
County Seat: Village of Jefferson
Named for: Native American word meaning "river of many fish"

Miles of Coast: 28 miles
Miles of Publicly Accessible Coast: 3.9 miles
Number of Access Sites: 11

Ashtabula County

A brief history:

Ashtabula County was formed on February 10, 1807, in Ohio's portion of the Connecticut Western Reserve. The original survey party, which first landed in the area of present-day Conneaut in 1796, was led by General Moses Cleaveland. Prior to Cleaveland's survey party traveling west to the area that would become the city named in his honor, one of Cleaveland's traveling companions, James Kingsbury and his family of five, remained behind in what would become Ashtabula County.

Ohio's largest county, Ashtabula's name is from an Iroquois word meaning "river of many fish." The land area covers almost 703 square miles; the southeastern corner lies outside of the Lake Erie Watershed.

Ashtabula County is overwhelmingly rural, but most residents earn their living by working in manufacturing, sales or service positions. Many people work in the shipping industry, transferring coal, iron ore and steel across the Great Lakes. Grapes are a popular crop owing to the favorable microclimate created by the lake; more than a dozen wineries are located in the county. During winter, Ashtabula County receives frequent and abundant lake effect snow and is part of the Southeastern Lake Erie Snowbelt.

In recent years, the county has experienced a small decline in population. The county seat is Jefferson; the largest is the coastal city of Ashtabula. Known for its abundance and variety of covered bridges, the county boasts more than any other Ohio county and is home to the longest covered bridge in the United States.

Learn More:

shtabula County
ww.co.ashtabula.oh.us

shtabula Area Chamber of Commerce
www.ashtabulachamber.net

shtabula County Covered Bridge Festival
www.coveredbridgefestival.org

shtabula County Metroparks
www.ashtabulacountymetroparks.org

shtabula County Visitors Bureau
www.visitashtabulacounty.com

shtabula Township
www.ashtabulatownship.com

ity of Ashtabula
.ashtabula.oh.us

ity of Conneaut
www.conneautohio.gov

onneaut Chamber of Commerce
www.conneautchamber.org

onneaut Port Authority
www.conneautportauthority.com

eneva Area Chamber of Commerce
ww.genevachamber.org

eneva Township
ww.genevatownshipohio.com

eneva-on-the-Lake
www.visitgenevaonthelake.com

aybrook Township
www.saybrooktownship.org

llage of North Kingsville
www.northkingsvilleohio.org

Public Access Management:

Local	8
Port Authority	2
State	1

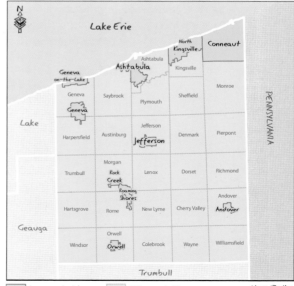

Geneva State Pa

Location:
Padanarum and
Lake roads
4499 Padanarum Road
Geneva-on-the-Lake,
OH

Latitude:
N 41° 50.77′

Longitude:
W 080° 58.46′

Waterbody:
Lake Erie

**Access
Site Type:**
Recreational

Environments:
Bluff
Riparian/River
Sandy Beach
Manmade Shore

The heavily-wooded 694.5-acre Geneva State Park is Ohio's easternmost state owned and managed coastal access site. It is located just west of downtown Geneva-on-the-Lake off State Route 534. The park can also be accessed from the east via Lake Road and from the south via Padanarum Road. The park's 1.6-mile shore includes scenic vistas, sand beaches, the park's marina entrance and the mouths of Wheeler and Cowles creeks.

A less than 20-foot wide sand beach fronts most of the park with exceptions near the 12 deluxe cedar cabins overlooking Lake Erie and near the marina. These areas are protected by shore structures. South of the cabins, Geneva's 100 camping sites are east of Wheeler Creek. A fish cleaning house is provided for campers.

The main Breakwater Swimming Beach extends more than 1,770 feet west from the marina's west breakwater and ranges from 200 feet to less than 50 feet wide. A portion of the beach is guarded. A bathhouse is near the beach's expansive parking lot.

Geneva's marina features 383 seasonal and transient docks, a 6-lane boat ramp, car-trailer parking and a concession supplying food, gasoline pumps, boating essentials and bait. The marina's 500-foot east breakwater is capped with a handicap-accessible sidewalk providing fishing access.

The Lodge and Conference Center at Geneva-on-the-Lake offers 109 guest rooms, a full-service restaurant, conference facilities and indoor and outdoor pools (for lodge guests only). The lodge is on the park's northeast side.

Hunting is seasonally permitted in designated areas. Additional park amenities include 8 miles of multi-use and paved trails, two shelter houses, and an archery range.

...k

Amenities and Services:

Location Map:

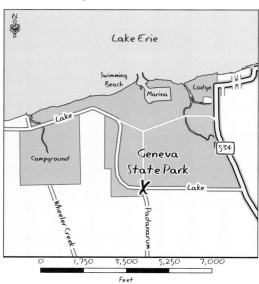

Lake Erie

Swimming Beach

Marina

Lodge

Lake

534

Campground

Geneva State Park

Lake

Wheeler Creek

Padanarum

| 0 | 1,750 | 3,500 | 5,250 | 7,000 |

Feet

Field Notes:

_____

_____

_____

_____

_____

_____

_____

_____

_____

_____

_____

_____

_____

_____

_____

_____

_____

Date Visited: _____

Learn More:
ODNR Division of Parks and Recreation
Geneva State Park
(440) 466-8400
ohiodnr.com/parks
ohiodnr.com/tabid/736/default.aspx

Ashtabula County

Geneva Township

Location:
Lake (SR 531) and Austin roads; secondary entrance at Old Lake Road Geneva-on-the-Lake, OH

Latitude:
N 41° 51.69'

Longitude:
W 080° 56.21'

Waterbody:
Lake Erie

Access Site Type:
Recreational

Environments:
Bluff
Sandy Beach
Manmade Shore

The 11.9-acre Geneva Township Park is north of State Route 531 (Lake Road East), east of Park Drive and west of the northern terminus of Austin Road. A parking lot is available north of Austin Road.

The bluff along the park's west has been gently graded to an easily-traversable mowed-grass slope. Ten precast concrete modular groins run along the west end of the park's 1,050-foot shore. Depending on water levels, a sand beach may be present between the groins. On the park's east, paved paths from the parking lot lead to a handicap-accessible wooden ramp which zigzags through natural-growth vegetation down the low bluff to a seawall. The seawall is capped with paved concrete. Fishing is allowed here as well as from the groins.

Benches overlooking Lake Erie are along the south side of a mulch path at the top of the bluff. The eastern portion of the park is partially shaded by deciduous trees while the west is an open mowed-grass field. Additional amenities at Geneva Township Park include picnic shelters and tables, playground equipment, trails, an upland sand volleyball court and a baseball field.

Swimming, camping, biking, skateboarding, alcoholic beverages, gambling and unleashed dogs are prohibited on park grounds. A bike rack is located at the park's main gate. Geneva Township Park is open form 9 am to dusk, May through September.

Ashtabula County

Park

Field Notes:

_____

_____

_____

_____

Amenities and Services:

_____

_____

_____

_____

_____

_____

Location Map:

N

Lake Erie

Geneva
Township Park
X

Old Lake
Park
Lake
531
Drummond
Fairfax
Austin
Hawley
Breen
Yale
Thomas
University
Kathryn
Linda

0   850   1,700   2,550   3,400

Feet

_____

_____

_____

_____

_____

_____

_____

_____

_____

_____

_____

_____

Date Visited: _____

Learn More:
Geneva-on-the-Lake
(440) 466-8600
www.visitgenevaonthelake.com

Ashtabula
County

Saybrook Towns[

Location:
State Route 531
near Russell Road
5941 Lake Road W
Saybrook Township,
OH

Latitude:
N 41° 52.64′

Longitude:
W 080° 52.58′

Waterbody:
Lake Erie

**Access
Site Type:**
Recreational

Environments:
Bluff

The 7.6-acre Saybrook Township Park is on State Route 531 (Lake Road West) east of the Russell Road intersection and west of the Mill Run Court intersection in Saybrook Township.

The day-use park has two large picnic shelters and a concession stand. The northern portion of the park is partially shaded by deciduous trees and has a large playground area at the center. A line of benches overlooking Lake Erie are just south of a wooden split-rail fence marking the northern extent of the park. Thick vegetation and a stand of trees cover a steep bluff to the shore. Access beyond the fence is prohibited.

Parking is available along the park's access road which runs a quarter-mile loop around the park. South of the access road the park has basketball and sand volleyball courts, an open mowed-grass green space and a baseball field.

The park is open dawn to dusk and year round, weather permitting.

ρ Park

Amenities and Services:

Location Map:

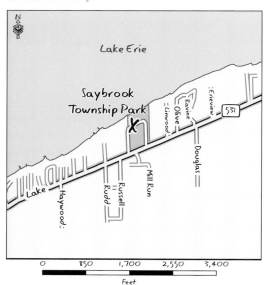

Lake Erie

Saybrook Township Park

531

Olive
Ravine
Erieview
Linwood
Douglas
Mill Run
Lake
Haywood
Russell
Rudd

N

0   850   1,700   2,550   3,400

Feet

Field Notes:

_____
_____
_____
_____
_____
_____
_____
_____
_____
_____
_____
_____
_____
_____
_____
_____
_____
_____
_____
_____
_____

Date Visited: _____

Learn More:
Saybrook Township
Saybrook Township Park
(440) 964-9177
www.saybrooktownship.org

Ashtabula County

Highland Beach

Location:
Walnut Boulevard and
Duquesne Avenue
Ashtabula, OH

Latitude:
N 41° 53.75′

Longitude:
W 080° 49.14′

Waterbody:
Lake Erie

**Access
Site Type:**
Scenic

Environments:
Bluff
Manmade Shore

The 3.2-acre Highland Beach is along Walnut Boulevard less than a quarter-mile north of the road's intersection with State Route 531 (Lake Road West). A neighborhood road, Duquesne Avenue, intersects Walnut Boulevard along the western third of the park.

This unsigned public access site has no beach. The 815-foot shore is protected by a stone revetment backed by a stepped concrete block seawall. A small amount of sand is impounded between the revetment and concrete blocks. The blocks provide a flat area to walk along and/or sit on at the base of the steep bluff.

The bluff is covered in thick vegetation which includes some small shrubs and trees. At the park's east end, a dirt path leads through a small stand of deciduous trees from the road down to the shore. A second dirt-grass path angles down the face of the bluff near the middle of the park.

The area of mowed grass at the top of the bluff is wider at the park's ends, averaging about 50 feet. However, for the majority of the park's 790-foot road length, the green space averages 20-feet wide. The park's only amenity is a single picnic table.

No parking is available at Highland Beach. By road, the park is 0.80 miles west of the city of Ashtabula's Walnut Beach Park.

Ashtabula
County

Field Notes:

_____

_____

_____

_____

Amenities and Services:

_____

_____

_____

_____

_____

Location Map:

_____

_____

_____

_____

_____

_____

_____

_____

Date Visited: _____

Learn More:
City of Ashtabula
Public Works
(440) 993-7036
www.cityofashtabula.com

Ashtabula
County

Walnut Beach Pa

Location:
Walnut Boulevard
and Lake Avenue
Ashtabula, OH

Latitude:
N 41° 54.08'

Longitude:
W 080° 48.32'

Waterbody:
Lake Erie

**Access
Site Type:**
Recreational

Environments:
Bluff
Dunes
Sandy Beach

The 28-acre Walnut Beach Park is at the terminus of Lake Avenue, north of the Walnut Boulevard intersection on the west side of Ashtabula River in the city of Ashtabula.

This coastal access site features a wildlife preserve, playground, beach volleyball courts, basketball courts, picnic tables, a skate park and concession stand. However, the majority of the city-owned park is an expansive foot-friendly sand beach backed by low dunes with beach vegetation.

Ashtabula Harbor's west breakwater is at the east end of the beach. It extends 1.4 miles into Lake Erie and provides fishing access. The Ashtabula Harbor Lighthouse is near the end of the limestone boulder breakwater.

From the foot of the breakwater, the city's public beach area extends nearly 800 feet west; the sand continues westward for another half-mile. Walnut Beach is approximately 500 feet at its widest area, which is just west of the parking.

In 1998 and 1999 city received Ohio Coastal Management Program grants for site improvements. The grants partially funded the construction of a handicap-accessible boardwalk and seating area, as well as a self-guided nature trail including observation decks and walkways over the beach dunes and estuary wetlands.

Walnut Beach is the northern terminus of the Great Ohio Lake-to-River Greenway. The park is adjacent to the north of Harbor-Topky Memorial Library and the Hubbard House Underground Railroad Museum; and adjacent to the west of the Ashtabula Coal Pier.

Ashtabula
County

...rk

Amenities and Services:

Location Map:

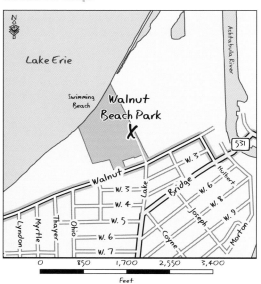

Lake Erie

Swimming
Beach

Walnut
Beach Park
X

531

Ashtabula River

Walnut

Lake

Bridge

Hulbert

W. 3

W. 6

W. 8

Joseph

W. 9

Coyne

Morton

W. 3

W. 4

W. 5

W. 6

W. 7

Lyndon

Myrtle

Thayer

Ohio

0   850   1,700   2,550   3,400

Feet

Field Notes:

_____
_____
_____
_____
_____
_____
_____
_____
_____
_____
_____
_____
_____
_____
_____
_____
_____
_____
_____
_____

Date Visited: _____

Learn More:
City of Ashtabula
Public Works
(440) 993-7036
www.cityofashtabula.com

Ashtabula
County

Lakeshore Park

Location:
State Route 531 and
State Road; access
also at East 1st Street
and Manola Avenue
1700 East 1st Street
Ashtabula and
Ashtabula Township,
OH

Latitude:
N 41° 54.34'

Longitude:
W 080° 46.46'

Waterbody:
Lake Erie

**Access
Site Type:**
Recreational

Environments:
Bluff
Sandy Beach
Manmade Shore

The 53.2-acre L-shaped Lakeshore Park is on the north side of State Route 531 (Lake Road East) and east of the Ashtabula River. The park's west end is north of the Minnesota Avenue terminus. The park's east end is north of the state road's intersection with Lake Road East and adjacent to the Ashtabula Power Plant.

Lakeshore Park's main access road, Lakeshore Drive, loops the park connecting the site's amenities. At the west end of the park's nearly half-mile waterline is a multi-lane boat launch. Fishing access is provided along this stretch of armored shore and from a 250-foot pier extending into Lake Erie.

East of the car-trailer parking lot is the 475-foot long Lakeshore Park Main Pavilion. Perched atop shore-adjacent green space, the pavilion is believed to be the longest and oldest Great Lakes pavilion in continuous use; historic photos are displayed in the pavilion.

The eastern 900 feet of shore is a groomed-sand swimming beach averaging 115 feet wide. In 1982, 34,000 cubic yards of sand were placed on the beach after the three 125-foot long, segmented, rubble-mound breakwaters were constructed to help stabilize the beach. A playground is at the back of the beach. The remaining park grounds are open to partially shaded mowed-grass green space. The park straddles land within the city of Ashtabula and Ashtabula Township and is managed by a township commission.

Field Notes:

_____

_____

_____

_____

_____

_____

_____

_____

Amenities and Services:

_____

_____

_____

_____

_____

_____

_____

_____

_____

_____

Location Map:

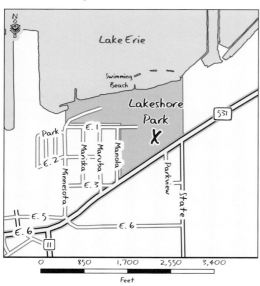

Date Visited: _____

Learn More:
Ashtabula Township
Ashtabula Township Park Commission
(440) 964-3819
www.lakeshoreparkashtabula.org

Ashtabula County

311

Al Cummings Sun

Location:
State Route 531 at
State Route 193
North Kingsville, OH

Latitude:
N 41° 55.63'

Longitude:
W 080° 41.48'

Waterbody:
Lake Erie

**Access
Site Type:**
Recreational

Environments:
Bluff

The 17.4-acre Al Cummings Sunset Park is located on land north of State Route 531(West Lake Road) with the park's entrance and parking area 0.4 miles east of the State Route 193 (North Main Street) intersection in North Kingsville.

This site includes partially-shaded mowed-grass green space and a lush wooded area. The gravel parking lot is accessible from a crescent-shaped drive off of State Route 531. The park's picnic shelter is adjacent to the parking area. Additional picnic tables are scattered throughout the park overlooking Lake Erie.

The top of the park's bluff is marked by a wooden split rail fence. This area of the coast has experienced significant erosion, and there is no beach at the base of the bluff. Due to the dangers of traversing the bluff and lack of amenities at the bottom, public access lakeward of the fence is prohibited.

Additional park amenities include playground equipment and natural trails leading through the woods. The Village Green Golf Course of North Kingsville is located on land south of State Route 531 across from the park.

Sunset Park is open daily from dawn to dusk.

Ashtabula
County

et Park

Location Map:

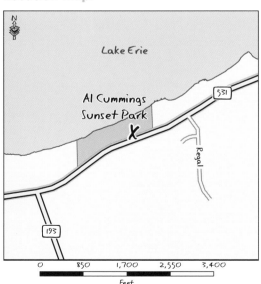

Lake Erie

Al Cummings
Sunset Park
X

531

Regal

193

| 0 | 850 | 1,700 | 2,550 | 3,400 |

Feet

Field Notes:

_____

_____

_____

_____

_____

_____

_____

_____

_____

_____

_____

_____

_____

_____

_____

_____

_____

Date Visited: _____

Learn More:
Village of North Kingsville
Parks and Recreation
(440) 224-0091
www.northkingsvilleohio.org

Ashtabula
County

Conneaut Town

The nearly 60-acre Conneaut Township Park is on land north of State Route 531 (Lake Road) from the Fairview Drive intersection east to Wrights Avenue. The park has numerous parking lots including lots off of the Chestnut Street Extension, and Grove Street's north terminus which loops the southeast corner of the park.

About half of Conneaut Township Park's acres are comprised of sand that has collected on the west side of Conneaut Harbor's west breakwater. The harbor's 0.3-mile long southern breakwater marks the east side of the beach. Sand covers all but the northern 600 feet of the breakwater, which is used for fishing access.

Extending west from this structure is the park's 0.4-mile long foot-friendly sand beach. It ranges in width from more than 1,000 feet along the east side to around 200-feet wide at the park's west end. A series of wooden boardwalks, collectively called the *Conneaut Township Park Boardwalk*, connect parking areas to the beach and shore.

The mouth of a small Lake Erie tributary crosses the middle of the beach. A wooden foot-bridge crosses the tributary. The beach also includes a small dune area.

In the upper park area, benches overlooking Lake Erie from atop a, tiered, grass-covered high bluff provide views of the harbor and Conneaut Harbor West Breakwater Lighthouse. Many additional park amenities are located in the upper park area including picnic facilities, playground equipment, a concession stand, athletic fields and courts

Ashtabula
County

hip Park

Amenities and Services:

Location Map:

N

Lake Erie

Conneaut Port
Authority Access

Swimming
Beach

Lakeview Park

Park

Erie

Conneaut
Township Park
X

Pearl

Fairview

Wrights

Lake

531

Walnut

Chestnut

Grove

Mill

Sandusky

Buffalo

Detroit

| 0 | 850 | 1,700 | 2,550 | 3,400 |

Feet

Date Visited: _____

Learn More:
City of Conneaut
Parks and Recycling
(440) 593-7430
www.conneautohio.gov

Ashtabula
County

Lakeview Park

Location:
Erie Avenue and
Sandusky Street
Conneaut, OH

Latitude:
N 41° 57.89'

Longitude:
W 080° 33.42'

Waterbody:
Lake Erie

**Access
Site Type:**
Recreational

Environments:
Bluff

The 8.7-acre Lakeview Park is at the northwest corner of Erie and Sandusky streets four blocks west of the Conneaut River in the city of Conneaut. The park is bounded on the north by Naylor Boulevard; Lakeview Park Drive loops through the southeast corner of the park.

Lakeview Park sits atop a high bluff and provides scenic vistas of Lake Erie, Conneaut Harbor and the Conneaut Harbor West Breakwater Lighthouse. Due to the accumulation of sand inside Conneaut Harbor's breakwaters, this coastal access site may appear to be an inland park. Park benches overlook the harbor and Lake Erie.

Lakeview Park is mostly mowed-grass green space with a few clusters of deciduous trees. The site features a picnic area, playground, baseball field and a basketball court.

Field Notes:

_____

_____

_____

_____

_____

_____

_____

_____

_____

Amenities and Services:

Location Map:

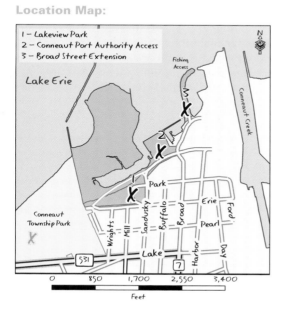

1 – Lakeview Park
2 – Conneaut Port Authority Access
3 – Broad Street Extension

Lake Erie

Conneaut Creek

Fishing Access

Conneaut Township Park

Park

Wrights Mill Sandusky Buffalo Broad Erie Pearl Ford Day

Lake Harbor

531 7

0   850   1,700   2,550   3,400
Feet

Date Visited: _____

Learn More:
City of Conneaut
Parks and Recycling
(440) 593-7430
www.conneautohio.gov

Ashtabula County

Conneaut Port A

Location:
Broad Street and
Park Avenue
Conneaut, OH

Latitude:
N 41° 58.03′

Longitude:
W 080° 33.29′

Waterbody:
Lake Erie

**Access
Site Type:**
Recreational

Environments:
Sandy Beach
Manmade Shore
Wetland

The 53.1-acre Conneaut Port Authority's Access is comprised mostly of accumulated sand and fill material. However, the boat launch/ fishing and walking pier area and the disjoined beach area appear as if they have always been a part of the inner areas of Conneaut Harbor.

The nearly 40-acre beach area has around 1 mile of waterline located east of Conneaut Harbor's west breakwaters. Massive amounts of sand have accumulated on both sides of the breakwaters with the sand in the inner harbor forming a vegetated boot-shaped oasis of trees, scrub-shrub and wetlands edged with a sand shore. The site is a very popular birding location. Foot-paths crisscross the inner areas of this sand peninsula. A wooden observation deck is onsite. Access to the beach is at the west terminus of the Naylor Boulevard/Erie Street intersection.

The Conneaut Port Authority has two launch ramps with a total of five lanes. Both ramps are located at the public docks on Naylor Boulevard. The fishing/walking pier's 800 feet of waterline surround an asphalt-paved parking lot with car-trailer spaces along the south and car only spaces to the north. A small area of green space with a few trees is near the lot's north end.

uthority Access

Amenities and Services:

Location Map:

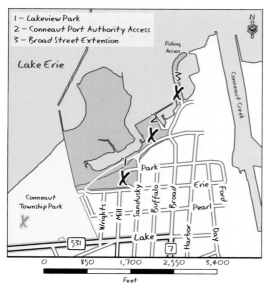

1 – Lakeview Park
2 – Conneaut Port Authority Access
3 – Broad Street Extension

Lake Erie

Fishing Access

Conneaut Creek

Conneaut Township Park

Park

Wrights
Mill
Sandusky
Buffalo
Broad
Erie
Pearl
Ford
Day
Harbor

Lake

531

7

0   850   1,700   2,550   3,400

Feet

Field Notes:

_____

_____

_____

_____

_____

_____

_____

_____

_____

_____

_____

_____

_____

_____

_____

_____

Date Visited: _____

Learn More:
Conneaut Port Authority
(440) 593-1300
www.conneautportauthority.com

Ashtabula County

Broad Street Ex

Location:
End of Broad Street,
north of Park Avenue
Conneaut, OH

Latitude:
N 41° 58.16'

Longitude:
W 080° 33.18'

Waterbody:
Lake Erie

**Access
Site Type:**
Impervious
Pier

Environments:
Manmade Shore

The Broad Street Extension is Ohio's easternmost public access site on Lake Erie. It is located to the north of the Naylor Boulevard and Marina Drive intersection, one block east of Lakeview Park.

This site is a nearly 1,000-foot J-shaped manmade breakwater that extends into Conneaut Harbor and serves as a popular fishing spot. Fishing is not permitted on the structure's east side as this is a private marina.

The Broad Street Extension is managed by the Conneaut Port Authority. The extension is adjacent to the north of Independence Park, a half-acre of partially-shaded green space.

~ension

Location Map:

1 – Lakeview Park
2 – Conneaut Port Authority Access
3 – Broad Street Extension

Lake Erie

Fishing Access

Conneaut Creek

N

Park

Conneaut Township Park

Wrights
Mill
Sandusky
Buffalo
Broad
Erie
Ford
Pearl
Harbor
Day

Lake

531

7

| 0 | 850 | 1,700 | 2,550 | 3,400 |

Feet

Field Notes:

_____
_____
_____
_____
_____
_____
_____
_____
_____
_____
_____
_____
_____
_____
_____
_____
_____
_____
_____
_____
_____
_____

Date Visited: _____

Learn More:
Conneaut Port Authority
(440) 593-1300
www.conneautportauthority.com

Ashtabula County

Acknowledgements

Principal Contributors, in alphabetical order:

Shaun Casbarro, ODNR Office of External Affairs – layout editor, design specialist
shaun.casbarro@dnr.state.oh.us

Brenda Culler, ODNR Office of Coastal Management – photographer, writer, reviewer, editor, webpage layout
brenda.culler@dnr.state.oh.us

Brian George, ODNR Office of Coastal Management – project manager, map production, fieldwork/data collection and verification, photographer, writer, reviewer, editor
brian.george@dnr.state.oh.us

Thanks to the dedicated Office of Coastal Management staff for proofreading, reviewing, assistance and support. Thanks also to all of our coastal partners, listed below, who provided significant assistance and feedback in the development of this guidebook.

Additional ODNR Photography Credits:

Karen Beckman, ODNR Division of Parks and Recreation

Ina Brolis, ODNR Division of Parks and Recreation

Mike Williams, ODNR Division of Mineral Resources Management

Gene Wright, ODNR Office of Coastal Management

Thanks to:
Larry Advey, Madison Township
Chris Basting, City of Huron
Karen Beckman, ODNR Parks and Rec.
Joe Beno, City of Lakewood
Robert Berner, City of Port Clinton
Mike Blakeman, ODNR Parks and Rec.
Amy Bowman-Moore, Erie MetroParks
Lisa Brohl, Black Swamp Conservatory, Lake Erie Islands Chapter
Ina Brolis, ODNR Parks and Recreation
Paul Buehrer, City of Oregon
Eileen Bulan, City of Vermilion

Scott Butterworth, ODNR Division of Wildlife
Susie Cooper, Lake Erie Islands Historical Society
Joyce Crease, Saybrook Township
Joe Dominick, City of Willowick
Scott Doty, ODNR Parks and Recreation
Dan Enovitch, City of Bay Village
Kelly Faris, Put-in-Bay Township
Tom Fattlar, City of Rocky River
Bill Gardner, City of Sheffield Lake
Dennis Garvin, City of Toledo
Larry Goedde, ODNR Division of Wildlife
Carrie Hansen, City of Cleveland
Bob Howland, City of Conneaut
Melinda Huntley, Ohio Sea Grant College Program
Jim Kastelic, Cleveland Metroparks
Lynn Kary, Village of North Perry
Vickie Kozak, Village of Marblehead
Jim Kidron, City of Lorain
Michelle Hall, City of Sandusky
Jim Hockaday, Village of Geneva-on-the-Lake
Dominic Iarocci, City of Ashtabula
Brian Katz, City of Willoughby
Douglas Leed, ODNR Division of Watercraft
Bryan Lucas, Village of Marblehead
Anne Maiden, City of Vermilion

Robert Martin, City of Mentor
Nan McBride, City of Oregon
Scott Miller, City of Sandusky
Kip Molenaar, City of Mentor-on-the-Lake
Alexandria Nichols, City of Avon Lake
Gary Obermiller, ODNR Division of Natural Areas and Preserves/Wildlife
Bobbie Oliver, Lake Metroparks
Michael Patterson, City of Rocky River
Tom Peters, Village of North Kingsville
Jim Schott, ODNR Division of Wildlife
James Seikel, ODNR Parks and Rec.
David Seman, City of Lakewood
Mike Semik, City of Eastlake
Walter Siegel, Perry Township
Richard Simon, Vermilion Township
Paul Snyder, Village of Bay View
Denver Spieldenner, Conneaut Port Authority
Dan Squires, City of Vermilion
Douglas Steinwart, City of Huron
Chris Trepal, Earth Day Coalition
Vince Urbanski, Lake Metroparks
Joe Wasserman, City of Oregon
Andy White, City of Huron
Debbie Woischke, ODNR Ohio Natural Heritage Program
Judith Yesso, Conneaut Port Authority